Fast Cycle

Organization

Development

A Fieldbook for
Organization Transformation

MERRILL C. ANDERSON, PH.D.
AND ASSOCIATES

South-Western College Publishing

an International Thomson Publishing company I(T)P®

Cincinnati • Albany • Boston • Detroit • Johannesburg • London • Madrid • Melbourne • Mexico City
New York • Pacific Grove • San Francisco • Scottsdale • Singapore • Tokyo • Toronto

Team Leader: Dave Shaut
Executive Editor: John Szilagyi
Marketing Manager: Rob Bloom
Production Editor: Kelly Keeler
Manufacturing Coordinator: Dana Schwartz
Internal Design: Jennifer Martin-Lambert
Production House: PublishWare
Printer: Webcom, Toronto, Ontario

I(T)P® The ITP logo is a registered trademark under license.

Printed in Canada

1 2 3 4 5 6 7 8 9 10

International Thomson Publishing Europe
Berkshire House
168-173 High Holborn
London, WC1V7AA, United Kingdon

Nelson ITP, Australia
102 Dodds Street
South Melbourne
Victoria 3205 Australia

Nelson Canada
1120 Birchmount Road
Scarborough, Ontario
Canada M1K 5G4

International Thomson Publishing Southern Africa
Building 18, Constantia Square
138 Sixteenth Road, P.O. Box 2459
Halfway House, 1685 South Africa

International Thomson Editores
Seneca, 53
Colonia Polanco
11560 México D.F. México

International Thomson Publishing Asia
60 Alberta Street #15-01
Albert Complex
Singapore 189969

International Thomson Publishing Japan
Hirakawa-cho Kyowa Building, 3F
2-2-1 Hirakawa-cho, Chiyoda-ku
Tokyo 102, Japan

You can request permission to use material from this text through the following phone and fax numbers:
telephone: 1-800-730-2214   fax: 1-800-730-2215
Or you can visit our web site at http://www.thomsonrights.com

Library of Congress Cataloging-in-Publication Data
Anderson, Merrill C.
    Fast cycle organization development : a fieldbook for organization
    transformation / Merrill C. Anderson and associates.
        p.   cm.
    Includes bibliographical references.
    ISBN 0-324-01328-0
    1. Organizational change. I. Title.
    HD58.8.A683 2000
    658.4′06--dc21   99-28180
                                                                CIP

This book is printed on acid-free recycled paper.

Preface

A recent newspaper article about a house built by Habitat for Humanity, the volunteer organization that builds high quality houses for lower income families, was noteworthy because of the *time* that it took the volunteers to build the house. In fact, they set a record time of four hours and 39 minutes! What was their secret for fast cycle house building? Their secret was to rethink the house building process and find ways to work in parallel rather than in a serial fashion.

A major challenge to organizational change practitioners is to fast-cycle the change process much as Habitat for Humanity has fast-cycled the house building process. Why does speed matter? Quite simply, it matters because business organizations have become time compressed and resource constrained. Business organizations can be leaders or fast followers—there is no prize for third place.

Organization change practitioners are reducing the cycle time of major change interventions by rethinking the traditional change process—diagnose, design, implement, evaluate, and enhance—and finding ways to accomplish these five steps in parallel rather than in a serial fashion. This is the essence of fast cycle organization development.

The intent of this book is to share some of the theory and practical applications of how to make change happen faster and better in organizations. The chapters are organized according to whether the change was primarily aimed at organizations, teams, or individuals. It is hoped that readers will have fun exploring these chapters, gain insights, and apply what they have learned to their own efforts to transform organizations.

Acknowledgments

Publishing a text is a team effort, and I have been fortunate to have been aided by a group of professionals at South-Western College Publishing. John Szilagyi, executive editor, shared with me the vision for the project and made sure the right people were in place to make it happen. Kelly Keeler, production editor, provided invaluable assistance in turning the manuscript into the book you now hold. Jennifer Martin added her creative talents for the overall design of the cover and interior. I would like to thank Rob Bloom, marketing manager, for his efforts in promoting the book. My wife, Dianna, superbly edited my contributions to this book, shaped my thinking, and supported me in so many ways. I am sure that I have tested her considerable talents as an executive coach many times over.

Merrill Anderson

About the Authors

Merrill Anderson is a management consultant with eighteen years experience maximizing the performance of organizations, teams, and people. He combines business-grounded pragmatism with extensive know-how in engaging people to create innovative business-focused solutions. Dr. Anderson has extensive experience as a learning and organization development consultant in both internal and external roles. He was formerly vice president of the Baxter Institute of Baxter Health Care Corporation. Prior to his position at Baxter, he was vice president, Organization Development, with NCR Corporation and director, Organization Capability Services, with Amoco Corporation. He began his career as a management consultant with Gemini Consulting, where he managed many major organization change engagements. Dr. Anderson is a dedicated educator and a member of the adjunct graduate faculty in organization development at Pepperdine University, Benedictine University, and Antioch University. He earned a Ph.D. in organizational studies at New York University and has over thirty professional presentations and publications to his credit. Mr. Anderson encourages dialogue with other organization change professionals and may be contacted through his e-mail address: merrilland@aol.com

Steven Cabana is co-author of *The Self-Managing Organization* and *The Search for Effective Strategic Planning is Over*. He wrote the first article in the United States on the Emery approach to redesigning organizations: "Participative Design Works, Partially Participative Doesn't." He is a graduate of the Gestalt Institute of Cleveland's Organization and System Development program and has sought to articulate contextual methods for changing large systems for fifteen years. His primary interest is in the application of the search conference and participative design methods for organizational renewal, growth, and innovation.

Bob Demaree is the supervisor of organization development for the Federal Mogul-Skokie facility (formerly Fel-Pro, Inc.), a worldwide automotive parts supplier. His consulting work focuses on the creation of productive workplaces by assisting business leaders, managers, and team leaders to identify and implement innovative business solutions through high performance teams, strategic planning, business process improvement, and technical training. Mr. Demaree has an M.S. in organization development from Loyola University, Chicago.

Merrelyn Emery is a lecturer at the Centre for Continuing Education at Australian National University in Canberra. Dr. Emery has conducted hundreds of search conferences throughout Australia, Europe, Canada, Central America, and the United States. Her pioneering efforts led to the first book published on theory of the search conference method, *Searching: For New Directions, in New Ways, for New Times.* Emery trains practitioners in the search conference and participative design methods at periodic seminars offered at the Institute for Resource Management at New Mexico State University in Las Cruces.

The late **Fred Emery** was a pre-eminent organizational psychologist, sociologist, and system theorist. Emery was associated with several companies that coupled social science research with action-based fieldwork to solve organizational problems. He was part of the first search conference for the merger of Bristol-Siddley Aircraft Engines in 1960. He did groundbreaking work on developing the key concepts of sociotechnical systems design. In the 1970s, Dr. Emery used the participative design methodology, a faster and more democratic approach to sociotechnical systems design. He was the author of dozens of books and articles dealing with organization design, social ecology, democracy, and systems theory.

Rodney Goelz is a senior organization development consultant with over 15 years experience managing organizations and coaching individuals through the human dynamics of change. He has a track record of providing thought leadership and driving improved performance results through the application of proven change management strategies and tactics. He is currently director of Associate Development within Worldwide Services Logistics (WSL) of NCR Corporation, based in Dayton, Ohio. Mr. Goelz has also led several transformational teams of professional services consultants for NCR, ranging from internally focused groups that pioneered new consultancy methods for worldwide use to externally focused teams that delivered change implementation assistance to Fortune 500 companies. Mr. Goelz holds a Bachelor's degree in business administration from Capital University, has a Master's degree in organization development from Bowling Green State University, has certification in ODR's

Managing Organizational Change® methodology, is certified in the use of the Myers-Briggs Personality Type Indicator, and is a certified facilitator in the Team Spirit process for developing high performing teams.

Barry Heermann is executive director of the Expanded Learning Institute. He is the creator of Team Spirit, a team development program that is delivered by organizational consultants nationwide in both profit and non-profit sectors. Dr. Heermann holds a Ph.D. from Ohio State University, an M.B.A. from the University of Dayton, and a B.S. from Bowling Green University. He has served as a consultant to over 250 organizations and has worked extensively in colleges and universities around the country. Dr. Heermann is a technical advisor, co-producer, and moderator of the PBS four-part series "Transitions," sponsored by the Kellogg Corporation. He has authored numerous articles on adult and experiential learning published in various national journals.

Bryan Law is a learning architect for Cerner Corporation, a medical software development company. Prior to joining Cerner, he was involved in human resources development work for 3M, Andersen Consulting Education, and AT&T Global Information Solutions. Mr. Law received his B.S. in education from the University of Minnesota and is currently enrolled in the M.B.A. program at the University of Missouri–Kansas City. He previously co-authored the Whole-Part-Whole Learning Model published in the *Performance Improvement Quarterly* journal.

Melinda Morrow is director for Organization Development at NCR Corporation, based in Dayton, Ohio. Her principal area of specialization is assessing an organization's capability to develop and execute its business strategy. She is also committed to consulting with leaders to move an organization and take appropriate actions for business success. Ms. Morrow holds certification in ODR's Managing Organizational Change® methodology, certification in the Myers-Briggs Type Indicator, and has experience as an internal consultant. In addition, she has consulting experience both domestically and internationally. She earned a Master's degree in organization development from Bowling Green State University and is a member of the OD Institute, the American Creativity Association, and the Organizational Development Professional Network.

Raymond Patchett is City Manager for the City of Carlsbad, California, where he has done extensive implementation and research of strategic change in public sector organization. He joined the City of Carlsbad in 1985 and served as Assistant City Manager until his appointment to City Manager in 1987. He has worked in local government since 1974 with the cities of Manhattan Beach, Redondo Beach, and Burbank.

Mr. Patchett holds a Master's degree in organizational development. He is a member of the Innovation Groups, the International City Manager's Association, and the California League of Cities.

Ronald Purser is associate professor of Management in the College of Business at San Francisco State University and an adjunct faculty member at Saybrook Institute, the California Institute for Integral Studies, and Benedictine University. Dr. Purser earned his Ph.D. in organizational behavior from the Weatherhead School of Management at Case Western Reserve University. He is co-author of *The Self-Managing Organization* and has published over 50 journal articles and book chapters on high performance work systems, design of new product development organizations, environmental management, social creativity, and participative strategic planning. Dr. Purser has been an active consultant and researcher in both the private and public sector.

Dick Richards is an organization development consultant, executive coach, team facilitator, trainer, and speaker. He has consulted with large and medium sized companies in the United States, Canada, Europe, Mexico, and Japan. His most recent projects involved organizations wanting to improve teamwork, develop leaders, encourage career self-reliance, or achieve world class customer service standards. Mr. Richards is the author of *Artful Work: Awakening Joy, Meaning, and Commitment in the Workplace,* which won the coveted Benjamin Franklin Award as best business book of 1996. He is a frequent contributor to professional journals and has appeared on many radio programs, such as *New Dimensions* and *Voice of America.*

Sander Smiles is a management consultant with expertise in the areas of strategic planning, business process design, team consulting, and change management assessments. Mr. Smiles has worked for the last ten years in organization development and adult learning. He most recently worked with Baxter Healthcare Corp. and previously worked as a mechanical engineer. Besides engineering, Mr. Smiles has completed graduate degrees in educational counseling and organization development.

Darryl Strickler has been involved in leading-edge projects in the cognitive sciences, organization learning, and human resource development for more than 25 years. As an independent consultant for the past 15 years, he has designed learning environments, produced informational/promotional and documentary-style video programs, and designed numerous multimedia and CD-ROM based systems. Dr. Strickler joined Baxter Healthcare Corporation in 1998 and serves as director of Learning and Performance Support.

Christopher Worley is associate professor of Business Strategy at Pepperdine University's Graziadio School of Business Management. His articles on strategic organization design have appeared in *The Journal of Organization Behavior,* the *International Journal of Public Administration,* and the *Project Management Journal.* He has presented to societies such as the Academy of Management, the Strategic Planning Forum, and the Conference Boards of Canada and the U.S. Individually and in collaboration with other firms, his consulting clients include organizations in high technology, financial services, health care, and public utilities. Dr. Worley received his Ph.D. in strategic management from the University of Southern California. He is a member of the Strategic Management Society, the Academy of Management, and the Organization Development Network.

Contents

P A R T *II*
Change Directed at the Organizational Level 29

P A R T *III*
Change Directed at Teams   67

P A R T *IV*
Change Directed at Individuals   89

P A R T *V*
Summary and Synthesis   107

Chapter 10
Lead With a Need for Speed   121

PART *I*

Foundations

Fast Cycle OD: "Faster, Better, Cheaper" Catches up to Organization Development

Merrill C. Anderson, Ph.D.

In recent years business organizations have faced unprecedented challenges to grow revenue, reduce operating costs, and invest in new product development and new market opportunities. Global competition is fierce. Speed of execution is paramount. Business organizations do not have the luxury of time to set a strategic direction and engage all employees in achieving strategic business goals. As a result, businesses have reduced cycle time in many aspects of their operations with innovations such as simultaneous engineering, lean manufacturing, and just-in-time inventory. The mantra of "faster, better, cheaper" guides many decisions to improve business operations.

Organization development practitioners have been designing and implementing organization change for the past fifty years. They have created a body of knowledge and skills that have proven to be invaluable to business leaders who have needed to implement organizational change. The OD value cycle—diagnose, design, deploy, evaluate, and enhance—represents proven methodology to implement change. However, OD does not operate in a vacuum, and the pressures that are operating on other aspects of the business are also impacting the practice of OD in business settings. Organizations have fewer people with less time to be engaged in organizational change. It is now time to reduce the cycle time of designing and implementing organizational change.

Fast Cycle OD represents a recognition of the global business reality that organizations face as well as a body of new interventions that are faster, better, and cheaper than more traditional OD interventions: *faster* in the sense that the steps of the OD value cycle are being collapsed and performed simultaneously and not in a serial fashion; *better* in the sense that these newer OD interventions deliver greater business value with a clearer line of sight to strategy; *cheaper* in the sense that less time to execute translates to greater return on investment.

The purpose of this chapter is to explore the concept of Fast Cycle Organization Development. Three trends accelerating how OD is practiced will be described and implications discussed for how these trends impact OD value creation for clients. The term "OD practitioner" refers to anyone whose primary role is implementing organizational change. Functionally, OD practitioners may be drawn not only from OD departments, but also from training and development, human resources, quality, and other functions. Ideally, line business managers would also have OD competencies in planning and deploying organizational change. This book is intended to share some OD tools, concepts, and business applications that exemplify fast cycle OD to a wide audience of OD practitioners and business leaders.

THREE TRENDS ACCELERATING THE CYCLE OF OD INTERVENTIONS

There are at least three major trends that are accelerating the pace at which OD creates value for business clients: First, the pace of business change is accelerating; second, OD interventions are increasingly engaging the *whole* client organization system; and third, OD is taking on an increasingly strategic focus. These three trends are depicted in Figure 1.1 as arrows accelerating the OD value cycle.

Pace of Business Change

Businesses operating in a globally integrated and highly complex economy have embraced *speed* as a key differentiator. Indeed, it is the sheer complexity of the emerging global economy that has placed even more emphasis on execution. The difference between winning and losing does not so much depend on who has the right strategy but rather who can execute the quickest. To paraphrase Jack Welsh, Chairman and CEO of General Electric, there are two kinds of people: those who try to predict the future and those who know they can't. Organizations that deal more effectively with present business realities will gain advantage in the market place. Organizations that refrain from taking action until the future can be accurately predicted and the right strategy can be formulated will inevitably lose.

FIGURE 1.1 *The Organization Development Value Cycle*

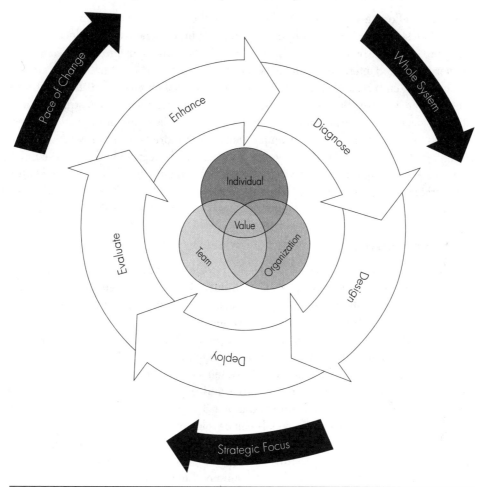

While knowing the future is not humanly possible, *preparing* the organization to meet future global challenges *is* possible. Organization development plays a critical role in changing or even transforming organizations so that these organizations are better prepared to meet global challenges. OD practitioners are discovering that playing this critical change role has required them to reinvent and reduce the cycle time of their change interventions. The mantra of "faster, better, cheaper" seems to have caught up with the practice of OD. Many business clients now expect OD practitioners to accomplish organization change objectives more quickly and more effectively with less investment of the organization's resources.

Whole System Interventions

OD change efforts are increasingly dealing with the *whole* client organization system rather than solely working on subsystem parts. OD practitioners and business leaders are approaching the organization as a complex, adaptive, and dynamic system composed of interrelated and interdependent elements: strategy, process, structure, people, reward mechanisms, culture, and other elements. Organizational change efforts now routinely include reengineering business processes, redesigning the organization structure, and aligning people and reward processes to fully support these organizational changes. Large system interventions, for example, organize hundreds of representatives from each unit of the client organization system into a highly integrated event. These interventions ensure that representatives from the whole organization interact in one (often very large) work space to bring the strategy and vision to life, explore organization design issues and alternatives, and align peoples' actions to achieve shared objectives.

Strategic Focus

The practice of OD is also becoming more strategic in nature. This trend also seems to reflect the increasing strategic focus of human resource management. Clients are expecting OD consultants to engage the entire client system and find more effective ways to execute strategy. Many business leaders cite their inability to effectively *execute* strategy as their biggest obstacle to success. OD is increasingly looked upon to help business leaders overcome this obstacle. Organizations are being viewed as complex and highly adaptive systems. Whole systems interventions, such as search conferences, reinforce a systems perspective and engage every constituency in an organization to co-create their future. Chapter 3 explores search conferencing as a strategic tool in detail. OD professionals can develop overarching change architectures that build the organization's capabilities to execute business strategy and better prepare the organization to successfully meet global competitive pressures.

The practice of formulating and communicating business strategy has in recent years become much more participative and open to people of all levels of the organization. No longer is strategy the exclusive preserve of senior executives gathering in corporate cloisters. The shelf life of business strategies has shortened. Strategies not quickly executed are of little value. The challenge is to *quickly* engage the hearts and minds of people in the organization to align their actions to the strategy and to do so as quickly as possible. Highly participative approaches to strategy development effectively merge strategy formulation, communication, and commitment activities. These approaches quickly create a foundation for strategy understanding and commitment, and therefore reduce the cycle time for overall strategy execution.

As strategy professionals become more concerned with engaging a diverse set of people in the organization to share in strategy formulation and as OD professionals become more focused on strategy execution, a natural and positive relationship between strategists and OD professionals is possible. In fact, not only is it possible, but each group's success—and business success—mutually depends upon their active collaboration. Strategists work with business leaders to make strategic choices about markets, technologies, products, assets, and so forth. OD practitioners craft and deploy interventions that engage all constituencies in the organization to digest these strategic choices and co-create their future. People develop ownership for the strategy they help create and more readily align their actions to the strategic direction of the business.

IMPLICATIONS FOR OD PRACTITIONER COMPETENCIES

There are three major sets of competencies that OD practitioners must have in order to be effective in strategy execution consulting. First, OD practitioners must speak the language of business and do so fluently. A basic understanding of finance and the theory and logic of financial decision-making is required. Second, OD practitioners must have a solid understanding of strategic formulation tools and conceptual models. Third, it is important for every OD consultant to do his or her business homework before beginning any client engagement: understand industry trends and issues, learn about the client company's history, explore the backgrounds of the leaders, and be able to articulate, at a minimum, the company's strategic intent, core competencies, competitive pressures, and market challenges. These represent some of the major "content" areas that OD practitioners are increasingly being called upon to create business value.

Another consequence of the pressure on OD to deliver the goods more quickly is that clients increasingly expect substantial *content* knowledge, not just process expertise, from their OD practitioner. It is no longer adequate to merely offer clients process facilitation services and eschew content. "Where's the beef?" is a commonly heard refrain. When an OD consultant is called upon to develop an executive team, for example, clients now expect the OD consultant to provide specific content regarding critical leadership competencies, offer industry knowledge on strategic leadership issues, and provide specific case study examples for benchmark comparisons with other companies. OD consultants are expected to be astute business professionals and offer astute business-related content knowledge.

There is a potential danger here of course. An OD consultant who offers too much in the way of content knowledge risks supplanting valuable client deliberations about what is important to the client's organization and strategy. These deliberations provide clients the opportunity to challenge their assumptions about the business, reframe their strategic issues, and develop creative new business approaches. Strategic deliberations offer a wealth of learning. Content knowledge should be introduced to stimulate learning and not supplant it.

VALUE CREATION

"Value" may be defined in this context as the creation of positive and lasting change that enables individuals, teams, and organizations to realize their full potentials and contribute to the success of the business enterprise. Enabling the execution of strategy and learning about how to improve the business are two primary ways that OD creates lasting value for business clients. The OD practitioner, the business clients, and many others work collaboratively to design and deploy a series of OD interventions. Each of these interventions must be linked to business strategy and explicitly identify at which level these interventions are primarily intended to impact: organization, team, or individual. Value creation for the business is accelerated by utilizing many interventions that address change at all three levels.

Transformative change requires change interventions to be simultaneously addressed at the individual, team, and organizational levels. Individuals in an organization, for example, may greatly expand their own learning, but if the work teams of which they are members do not fundamentally change the way they work together, then the "transformed" individual will quickly be reshaped and brought back into the corporate fold. Team norms exert tremendous influence. The team setting will actively discourage individuals who try to shake things up and try to perform new behaviors that they have learned. Team-building interventions that fundamentally shift team norms would additionally be required in this situation to embrace the new perspectives and new behaviors of the newly transformed individual.

Similarly, a work team that has learned to transform itself will not be able to sustain its new performance for long unless the organization's work process, power structure, HR policies, and other elements fully support the team's new perspectives and work habits. Organizational interventions would need to be conducted to allow all work teams to share in the same learnings and adopt the same practices as the newly transformed team. For example, strategic search conferences could be conducted that would engage all teams and constituencies in embracing new learnings and creating a new compelling vision of the future.

This book has organized some of the newest and most powerful OD interventions according to the primary level at which these interventions are addressed. Change at the organization level is addressed in Chapters 3 (search conferences) and 4 (organization redesign). Change at the team level is exemplified by Chapters 5 (Kaizen) and 6 (fostering team spirit). Change at the individual level is explored in Chapters 7 (fast cycle learning) and 8 (coaching). Chapter 9 presents a case study illustrating how an integrated approach featuring interventions directed at all three levels can achieve strategic change and outstanding business results. Chapter 10 discusses the role of leadership in times of tumultuous change.

THE OD VALUE CYCLE

OD professionals create positive and lasting value for their clients by following the five basic process steps outlined in the OD value cycle (see Figure 1.1). Most OD interventions include these five basic process steps. Of course, these basic steps may be taken in various sequences or compressed or combined in unique and creative ways. The point here is that successful OD interventions will feature each of these process steps. The essence of fast cycle OD is to accelerate how these steps are enacted by finding ways to reduce cycle time and by enacting these steps in parallel rather than tacitly following them in a sequential fashion. Briefly reviewing each of the steps in the OD value cycle will clarify how OD interventions are conducted, as well as to provide some insights into how OD professionals are reducing their cycle time to create lasting value for client organizations.

Diagnosis

Diagnosis of individuals, teams, and the organization is the first step. The intention for this diagnosis is to enable people to learn about themselves, their teams, and their organizations. OD practitioners will engage representatives from many (if not all) of the relevant constituencies and stakeholders to conduct a series of analyses. All relevant and available data will be reviewed, such as organizational surveys, investor reports, annual reports, strategy documents, and other information. Internal best practices can be discovered and documented at this point. Customized surveys, focus groups, executive interviews, and other probes can be developed and fielded as necessary. The end result of the analysis is to understand the organization (its strategy, processes, structure, and so forth), its business context (markets and competition), and major improvement opportunities (e.g., improving the business sales process, reducing fixed costs associated with support work, and the like). Also, these analyses are conducted and results communicated in such a way that the entire organization understands and buys into the rationale and the context for change.

Communication is a key ingredient. A foundation for understanding, acceptance and ownership of the proposed organization change must be established as early as possible. Key messages must be crafted and shared with all organization constituencies. Measures must also be taken to ensure *comprehension* and not just communication. Often, messages must be communicated several times in several ways to ensure full comprehension by all constituencies.

Design

The next step in the value cycle is to work with the client organization to design an appropriate series of interventions. These interventions address the improvement opportunities—or at least provide some direction as to how these improvement opportunities will be addressed. OD consultants and clients agree on the change out-comes and objectives, resource requirements, project deliverables, and their respective responsibilities in the change effort. Very often a Gantt chart and project approach will be developed that will help manage the change effort. The project approach will outline each intervention, its scope, sequencing, timing, and resource requirements. The design of the change effort will be flexible to allow ample midcourse corrections.

Deployment

Deployment refers to the OD consultant and client co-implementing the agreed upon interventions. Very often a joint consultant/client change team is formed. This team leverages the skills, knowledge, and abilities of the consultant while also facilitating transfer of thought leadership from the consultant to the client organization. The progress of deployment is reviewed on a regular basis by the joint change team and by the client leadership team(s). Successes are celebrated and problems are discussed and corrected in real time.

Evaluation

The deployment of change interventions is formally evaluated. Internal best practices are highlighted and documented. Various client groups are formed to determine what worked well and what lessons were learned in the process of change. Surveys, focus groups, interviews, and other methods of data collection that were fielded in the di-agnosis phase can be refielded to provide a prepost trend analysis.

Another critical aspect of evaluation is to determine the business impact and the return on the investment that the business leaders made in the change effort. Busi-ness impact refers to the measurement of the impact that the change interventions had on operational performance. For example, a change effort designed to improve in-ventory management would presumably impact inventory turns and return-on-asset measurements. Return on investment is expressed as a ratio of financial benefits that the client realized as a direct result of the change intervention to the amount of money that the client had to invest in order to produce these financial benefits. Chapter 9 ex-plains in more detail how these calculations can be made.

It is also essential at this point for the change team to reflect upon their role in the change process. Change team members are engaged in dialogue to better understand how their mental models shape their perceptions, influence their actions, and contribute to determining project outcomes. This represents key learning for OD practitioners to help them improve and hone their skills and incorporate new knowledge and new learnings into their practice of OD. This is an essential step for building personal mastery.

Lines of inquiry that can be utilized to gain further insight into the change process include: What was learned about the process of change? What did the clients learn about themselves? How well were the learnings harvested and shared across organizational boundaries? The insight gained from answering these questions may be utilized to enhance not only the effectiveness of the implementation effort but also the effectiveness of the change intervention methodology.

Enhance

The critical evaluation of the change effort provides a foundation for continuous improvement of the business organization as well as improving how change is conceived and executed. Best demonstrated practices can be expanded throughout the organization. Lessons learned can be translated into change management practices. New opportunities for operational improvements can be acted upon. The OD value cycle then repeats as new change initiatives are designed and launched. This is how new ways of creating value are discovered and the learning process continues.

Value is created for clients at each step of the value cycle. Diagnosis enables clients to develop new insights into their business. Designing a *change architecture* provides clients with a sense of the "big picture" and how each business unit contributes to the whole enterprise. Deployment of the change creates lasting improvements in the business organization and also builds strategy execution skills, leadership abilities, and organizational knowledge of those who are involved in the change. Evaluating what went well and what went poorly opens up opportunities for reward, recognition and learning valuable lessons. Enhancing the learning capability of the organization may be the greatest gift of all. Ideally, enacting and accelerating the OD value cycle becomes a continuous and natural way that the organization operates. People continue to learn, the organization continues to grow, and business results become even more spectacular.

THE PRACTICE OF FAST CYCLE OD

In today's global business environment business leaders must accelerate strategy execution, and OD practitioners must accelerate how they add value in the eyes of business leaders. Ways must be found to accelerate the OD value cycle. Conducting two or more of the five cycle steps simultaneously, rather than sequentially, is a powerful way to accelerate change. This reduces the cycle time. Multigeneration organization design (Chapter 4) blends design and deployment to accelerate change. Kaizen (Chapter 5) rapidly accelerates the entire cycle. Fast cycle learning (Chapter 7) utilizes ethnographic analysis to improve diagnosis and design of learning interventions.

The authors hope that readers will utilize this book to gain greater clarity and insight into executing organizational change and apply the concepts, tools, and methodologies to their own work. Each chapter offers a unique theoretical perspective or an innovative methodology (or both) that elaborates on the concept of Fast Cycle OD. While there is no cookbook on how to practice OD, the final two chapters attempt to provide some sense of how all of the pieces can be fit together to successfully execute strategic change. It is hoped that readers will find some helpful ways of thinking about their work and find some useful tools and methodologies to bring added value to their business clients.

SUGGESTED READINGS

To better understand the evolving practice of OD:

Anderson, M. C., August, J., & London, J. (1995). Insights from OD best practices pilot survey: guiding the start-up of an internal OD team. *Organization Development Journal 13*(3), 57–65.

Bunker, B., & Alban, B. (1996). *Large Group Interventions*, San Francisco: Jossey-Bass.

Lawler, E. E., & Galbraith, J. R. (1993). New roles for staff: strategic support and services. In J. R. Galbraith & E. E. Lawler (Eds.), *Organizing for the Future*. San Francisco: Jossey-Bass.

McMahan, G. C., & Woodman, R. W. (1992). The current practice of organization development within the firm: a survey of the 500 largest industries. *Group and Organization Management 17*, 117–134.

Mohrman, A. M., & Lawler, E. E. (1993). Human resource management: Building a strategic partnership." In J. R. Galbraith & E. E. Lawler (Eds.), *Organizing for the Future*, San Francisco: Jossey-Bass.

To better understand the foundations of strategic thinking and the latest trends in the practice of strategy formulation:

Byrne, D. (1996). Strategic planning. *Business Week*, August 26.

Galagan, P. A. (1997). Strategic planning is back. *Training and Development Journal*, April.

Hamel, G., & Prahalad, C. K. (1994). *Competing for the future*, Boston: Harvard Business School.

Porter, M. E. (1980). *Competitive strategy*, New York: The Free Press.

Myth and Hope Meet Reality: The Fallacy of and Opportunities for Reducing Cycle Time in Strategic Change

Christopher G. Worley
and Raymond R. Patchett

I t never fails. The client is facing an important challenge by a competitor in one of their key product/market areas. They have asked for help in formulating a response to this threat. Is their strategy correct, should it be adopted, and if so, what organization changes are necessary to implement the new strategy? A number of presentations and discussions suggest that you and the client can see how such a process might unfold. And then it happens. The client asks, "How long do you think this will take?" Silence. In your best-trained voice you say, "Most changes of this type take two to three years." Silence. The client fidgets. She's uncomfortable. You can feel the frustration in the room. What you are proposing doesn't fit with her view of what needs to happen quickly.

The scenario is not much different in the public sector. Citizen demand for rapid governmental response to pressing issues and threats to vote out unresponsive politicians lead city councils to quickly announce new policies aimed at holding public employees accountable for their performance. Implementation drags. The new policies attack the heart of the bureaucratic culture that resists change. Expecting an immediate response, the council expresses frustration and asks for patience on the part of voters.

These scenarios are being played out with increasing frequency. Managers sense an urgency to formulate and implement strategic changes more quickly. In the jargon of the month, they want a "faster cycle time." In this chapter, an interpretation of "fast cycle time strategic change" is supported by case descriptions, and the implication of such a phrase is clarified. These monikers imply a type of change that may conspire with and coop managers into believing that large-scale change can happen quickly. The truth is, it cannot. While certain phases and activities during the strategic change process can be accelerated, other phases cannot.

The chapter begins by defining strategic orientation, cycle time, and the process of strategic change. In the second section, opportunities are explored for decreased cycle time in the strategic change process. Case examples illustrate both potential and constraint. Finally, some conclusions are drawn, and how these conclusions might be applied to facilitate the psychological and tangible aspects of strategic change is discussed.

DEFINITIONS

This section defines an organization's strategic orientation, describes the concept of cycle time, and applies it to the process of strategic change.

Strategic Orientation

A strategic orientation refers to the strategy and organization design that defines the relationship between an organization and its environment. It describes the context of organization members' experiences as well as the "what" of strategic change. Strategy refers to the organization's mission, goals, strategic intent, key policies around research and development, marketing, human resource development, and finances. The organization design includes the structure, information systems, work design, and human resource systems that support the strategy and facilitate its implementation.

Together, strategy and organization design make up a strategic orientation. Separating strategy from organization design often facilitates thinking about strategic change, but the research is clear that the two move together and that their alignment is a key element in performance and effectiveness.

Cycle Time

Cycle time refers to the interval bounded by the initial steps and concluding activities of a process or routine. For example, new product development processes describe the activities that bring a product or service concept to market. The cycle time represents the number of days, weeks, or months that elapse from the time a commitment to the concept is made and the time it is offered to customers. Reducing cycle time is an important element in popular interventions, such as total quality management and business process reengineering.

Fast cycle strategic change, then, refers to the amount of time required to complete the process of strategic change. Therein lies the rub. What is the process of strategic change and what opportunities are available to reduce the cycle time?

The Process of Strategic Change

Strategic change definitions need to address not only what to change, but how and when to change different elements of a strategic orientation. "Strategic change" is defined here as the deliberate and coordinated processes that lead to *systemic* realignments between the environment and a firm's strategic orientation, and which result in improvements in performance and effectiveness. This definition suggests that there are causes and consequences to change, that the content of change is defined by alterations in an organization's strategic orientation, and that strategic change is a process. At the present time, however, there are no clearly accepted strategic change process steps. Four different processes are shown in Table 2.1.

Traditional models of strategic management suggest that strategies and organization designs evolve through cycles of formulation and implementation. The formulation process involves (1) understanding the organization's strengths and weaknesses, its opportunities and threats, its distinctive competencies, and its vision of the future; and (2) proposing a set of goals to achieve and the plans to achieve them. The implementation phase generally follows formulation and involves arranging the structure and control systems necessary to bring the strategy into reality. In comparison with formulation, strategy implementation historically has received less attention.

Several more specific strategic change models have been proposed. One proposal suggests that strategic change is initiated by new, outside CEOs brought in to implement change. Quickly, the CEO acts to solve short-term performance problems and consolidate power. Jan Carlzon's turnaround at SAS Airlines is a good example. The CEO then develops a consensus among the top management team on strategic direction, and realigns the organization's structure with supporters filling key positions. Finally, leadership responsibility is transferred to middle managers, and new systems are implemented to assure consistency in workforce behavior.

Another researcher suggests that within the context of internal forces resisting change and external forces promoting change, senior managers interpret their environments and, if appropriate, commit to strategic change. In the second phase, the firm revises its strategic posture to gain new competitive advantages at the business level, to extend core capabilities at the corporate level, or to broaden a network of alliances at the collective level. Finally, managers energize strategic change. This involves redefining the organization's vision, allocating resources toward new

TABLE 2.1 *Models of Strategic Change*

Strategic Change Process	Steps or Phases
Traditional Strategic Management	• Formulation • Implementation
Greiner and Bhambri, 1989	• New, outside CEO • Short-term performance improvement • Power consolidation • Consensus building • Restructuring • Decentralization
Fombrun, 1992	• Environmental scanning • Commitment to change • Revising strategy • Energizing change
Worley, Hitchin, and Ross, 1996	• Strategic analysis • Strategy making • Strategic change plan design • Strategic change plan implementation

directions, modifying organizational systems, and generating commitment among organizational members.

These two examples demonstrate the difficulty in establishing a strategic change process definition. The first example is primarily concerned with internal processes of power and structure, while the second example is primarily concerned with external issues of competitive advantage and positioning. In addition, each example differs in the timing and sequence of changes in strategy, structure, vision, and other elements of strategic orientation.

The final approach differs from the others by suggesting that organization development can provide value-added insights into the process of strategic change. The first step is strategic analysis, or diagnosis of the current strategic orientation. This is followed by strategy making, or the specification of a desired future strategic orientation. A third step involves designing an agenda for change that sets the organization on a path toward the new strategic orientation and then implements that agenda.

What many models of strategic change share in common is that the organization exists in a present state, desires to achieve some future state, and implements actions to bring that change about. What is different about newer models of strategic change, reflecting an interest in decreasing the cycle time, is an attempt to move from the present to the future state more quickly. These models eschew the "transition state" and suggest that following a visioning process, the organization should move directly to the future state.

SOURCES OF CYCLE TIME REDUCTION

What opportunities and constraints exist in accelerating the process of strategic change? This section suggests that strategic change, like other routines and processes, is amenable to cycle time improvement. We also want to suggest that there are limits to this improvement. Just performing the same processes more quickly often detracts from quality or cost. To perform the process more quickly, the process itself must be changed. When strategic change is looked at as a process or flow of activities, there are at least two sources of decreased cycle time: executing particular phases in new ways and organization learning.

Reduce Cycle Time Through More Efficient Execution of the Individual Phases

As described above, the process of strategic change consists of several phases, such as strategy making or implementation. Each phase typically involves several steps, such as performing market research, determining the organization's distinctive competencies, or analyzing the capital requirements for a new facility. In general, the more steps within a phase, the more difficult the coordination task, the more costly the processes, and the longer the change will take. Table 2.2 displays the phases of strategic change. For each phase, there is a purpose, keys to success, and intervention opportunities. Cycle time can be reduced by performing each phase more quickly and by combining steps within a phase into one integrated process.

Strategic Analysis

The purpose of strategic analysis is to understand the current strategic orientation. A thorough diagnosis of the existing organization generates important information about what can and cannot be implemented; what will or will not be supported by the organization's culture. The keys to success include broad participation and building commitment to change. The strategic analysis process subscribes to the "go slow to go fast" principle. By involving members in understanding the current organization's strengths and weaknesses, there is less resistance during implementation, and thus the overall cycle time of strategic change is reduced.

TABLE 2.2 *Criteria and Interventions to Accelerate Strategic Change*

	Strategic Analysis	*Strategy Making*	*Designing the Strategic Change Agenda*	*Implementing the Strategic Change Agenda*
Purpose	*Diagnosis*	*Formulation*	*Set the Stage*	*Do the Work*
Keys to Success	• Broad participation • Building commitment to change	• Make clear choices • Be systemic • Don't get mired in detail	• Broad participation • Don't get mired in detail • Establish the why	• Making the vision real • Providing resources and support • Controlling the process
Interventions for Acceleration	• Large-group conferences	• Limit participation • Top team readiness • Clarify values	• Large-group conferences	• Concurrent scheduling

However, that doesn't mean the diagnosis has to take a long time. Recent developments in large-group methodologies permit this step to be completed rather quickly.

For example, a legal book publisher's strategic analysis process was greatly accelerated by a large-group conference. An important new technology (CD-ROM) was threatening the organization's long held reputation and market share advantages. To better understand the competitive conditions and the organization's fitness to respond, the executive team convened a "high-involvement SWOT" conference. Customers, field sales representatives, editors, production managers, and internal technology experts were invited to a two-day workshop that identified the organization's strengths, weaknesses, opportunities, and threats. Only two weeks were required from the decision to initiate the strategic planning process to the end of the two-day conference. Two additional days of staff time were required to document the learnings from the conference.

The high-involvement SWOT produced a large volume of high quality information that quickly brought out the key issues and priorities. Participation from a broad spectrum of stakeholders and organization members exposed them to the complexity of the problem, and built consensus around the need for a strategic response.

Strategy Making

The purpose of the strategy making process is to formulate the desired future strategy and organization design. The keys to success include making clear choices, being systemic, and not getting mired in detail. Organizations must make clear choices about the different components of strategic orientation. Two interventions that can facilitate these choices are values clarification and top management team building. Values clarification interventions help the organization sort out what is important and prevent it from "spinning its wheels." For example, lengthy and frustrating discussions about different organization design elements, key assumptions of strategy, or about whether goals should be set higher or lower are often values discussions cloaked in organizational and financial language. If senior management is clear about the organization's values, important choices can be made more quickly. Similarly, team-building interventions can result in senior management teams that are better equipped to make crisp, reasonable decisions with regard to the organization's future state.

The second and third keys to success in this phase are being systemic and not getting mired in detail. A good strategy formulation process produces a full description of the strategy and organization design systems that together must support the strategy. By taking a high-level look at these systems, and not specifying every detail of the future state, strategic, as opposed to tactical, issues are identified more quickly. An organization's future strategic orientation is too complex a phenomenon to describe in detail. Moreover, the implementation process that follows is too uncertain to warrant specification of each aspect of the future state.

Thus, the key source of cycle time reduction in strategy making is to limit participation. Too often, organizations (and the OD practitioners that advise them) believe that every part of a change process must be high involvement in nature. This is not true. It is important to involve members at key times. Too much participation at this stage of change dilutes the power and advantages of a bold strategy and inevitably lengthens the process as different functional groups or stakeholders consciously or unconsciously push for favored goals, strategies, and systems' characteristics. The result is a weak strategy and industry average (or worse) performance. Limited participation facilitates being systemic and not letting details become the focus.

The legal book publisher worked through the issues of its future strategy and organization quickly. Two weeks after the high-involvement SWOT, the senior managers met for a three-day strategy workshop. Intense discussions over the organization's "driving force" and its mission produced clear criteria for decisions. The most difficult discussion revolved around the aggressiveness of the new CD-ROM product goals and the implications on other product lines. Based on the relative urgency suggested by the goals for each product line, the team confirmed their strategic intent; examined, established, or changed key policies; and outlined organization design elements required to support the new strategy. Finally, important initial tactics were developed.

The publishing case clearly shows that important and substantive work on strategic change can occur in short periods of time. The total time from initiation of the strategic change process, to a clear sense of the organization's future state and the key tactics necessary to get there, was just over four weeks.

Designing the Strategic Change Agenda

The purpose of this phase is to set the stage for implementation. The keys to success include broad participation, establishing the "why," and not getting overwhelmed with details. Again, large-group methods can play an important role. For example, the City of Carlsbad, California, engaged in a strategic change process following four years of recession, downsizing, and difficult labor relations. As the economy improved, the city began to take steps to reenergize itself. Following processes of analysis and strategy making, the city organized a two-day "futuring conference" to gain commitment and support for the city's new strategy. More than 120 city employees attended from all service areas and levels of the organization. The participants discussed and refined vision, mission, and values statements. Based on this direction, the group developed more than twenty strategic initiatives to move it to the future state. The initiatives were sorted into six areas: systems and structures, communication, employee excellence, customer service, technology and resources, and fiscal stability. Groups of participants evaluated, prioritized, and recommended action regarding the areas.

Thus, designing a strategic change plan does not require long periods of time. In addition, the large-group method allowed the organization to stay at an appropriate level of analysis and not get bogged down in details. Finally, by reviewing the mission, vision, and values, participants and representatives from the organization were able to understand the context of their work and why the initiatives were being developed.

Implementing the Strategic Change Agenda

The purpose of implementation is to bring the desired future state into reality. This is the least talked about aspect of strategic change. Most OD and strategic management processes focus on the formulation stages, leaving implementation activities as after-thoughts. The keys to successful implementation include making the vision real, providing resources and support, and controlling the process. *Making the vision real* means constantly reminding organization members of the business case for change, setting high and positive expectations about new behaviors, and giving members permission to act in new ways. It sends powerful symbolic messages that the future is now. *Providing resources and support* means allocating time and money to key projects that push change forward, and that doing things in a new way is valued. *Controlling the process* recognizes that change unfolds over time and cannot be pre-programmed. Leadership must be alert to solving problems as they emerge, celebrating success, and making change stick by formalizing important elements of a new strategic orientation.

Of all the phases in the strategic change process, implementation is the least amenable to acceleration. The uncertainty involved in modifying a strategic orientation prevents specifying, in advance, all of the activities and tactics required to bring the future state into reality. Thus, speed in designing the change agenda makes sense because large-scale change is unprogrammable. Successful implementation means working within the new design and getting people to carry out activities differently. In other words, the only way to change behavior is to change behavior. People do not just drop old ways of doing things and become proficient at new behaviors without some learning cost. During change, organization members move from places of competence to incompetence and from knowing how to do something to having to learn something new. As the new way of working and organizing becomes better understood with experience, new change opportunities emerge that were not apparent earlier and must be addressed. The new requirements thwart any preconceived notion of how long a change will take. If the desired state is to become reality, people must learn to do the organization's work in a new way—and learning takes time. Thus, it is very difficult to speed up the process of implementation.

One option, concurrent implementation tracks, can accelerate organization change on many levels. It allows different projects to be implemented simultaneously. This is being attempted by Carlsbad. Following the futuring conference, the city manager reprioritized already scarce resources to the systems and structure, to the communications process, and to the employee excellence initiatives. All three were launched at the same time. Even as these changes were being started, the city was orchestrating a major information systems implementation. The customer service, technology and resources, and financial stability teams were scheduled to begin their work later. Thus, if the senior leadership in an organization can take a bird's-eye view of the implementation pieces, it is possible to reduce the amount of time required for implementation, although doing so entails considerable risk.

Foremost among these risks is the difficulty in coordinating multiple concurrent projects and cost. Not every organization can afford to allocate enough time, money, and people to several change projects and still accomplish the work of the organization. Similarly, not every organization possesses the project management and change management skills and knowledge to coordinate highly interdependent projects.

Reduce Cycle Time by Learning to Perform Change Better Each Time

Another source of cycle time reduction, one with an eye toward the long-term viability of the organization, is to look at strategic change as a recurring cycle, not a one-time sequence of activities. Strategic change is an important time in an organization's life, but it is not an isolated event. Organizations that prosper for long periods of time, such as Hewlett-Packard and General Electric, must execute these substantive changes over and over again. Since the process of strategic change is a recurring one, organizations would do well to develop the skills and abilities, routines, and competencies that allow it to make important strategic changes when needed. This too is an important source of cycle time reduction.

During and after a strategic change process, managers and consultants can examine what worked and what did not work. They can examine where there were delays, postponements, or lost momentum. For example, early experiences with the large-group conference methodologies demonstrated that particular segments of the process could be shortened. However, the conference was often viewed as an event, not as part of the process. As a result, some aspects of strategy formulation were performed quickly, but there were big "letdowns" following the conference. The organization was unprepared for the momentum created by the conference. As owners of the change process were getting tooled up for the next phase, the psychological momentum and commitment built up by the conference was dissipated and lost in the organization's membership. An organization's real strength, and competitive advantage, lies in the skills and ability of its members to learn over and over again.

Unfortunately, organizations, under pressure to produce goods and services faster, better, and cheaper, often believe they have little time to reflect on overall processes of strategic change. In most organizations, this is not considered a value-added activity. It has led to the disappointing conclusion by Argyris and Schon that there are no "learning organizations."

CONCLUSIONS

The purpose of this chapter was to explore the concept of cycle time in the context of strategic change. Arguments and case examples suggested that certain parts of strategic change can be accelerated while other parts cannot. They also suggested that an organization learning perspective also holds significant promise. This data points to three conclusions. First, successful strategic change requires facing organizational and personal dilemmas. Second, it is important that OD practitioners and client systems are clear about what "fast cycle time" means during strategic change. And third, organizations do not recognize the value of learning in cycle time reduction.

Facing Dilemmas

At the organizational level, successfully implementing strategic change requires constantly balancing the dilemma posed by one's enthusiasm to move forward quickly with the reality that the organization mass moves at its own pace. Finding a tempo that does not move too fast or too slow, and that maintains the momentum and commitment to change, is critical to successful implementation at any speed. In both the book publishing and the city government examples, senior managers continually received feedback from the organization that the pace of change and the amount of work generated by the change process were overwhelming. Managers and employees expressed concern, sometimes with frustration and anger, about not having time to do their work and spending too much time in meetings. On the other hand, the OD consultants repeatedly advised management that the process needed to move quickly in order to maintain the momentum. The reality is that both organization members and the OD consultants are correct.

Facing the dilemma of balancing the daily operational workload with the activities required to implement the change process proves to be an ongoing leadership and organization challenge. Finding the most effective pace for organization change means being able to make choices among ongoing operational demands, intervention implementation, and the stress each creates on the organization's people and its systems. The goal is to create enough tension in the organization to keep it moving forward without creating high levels of resistance and stress that could impede the change process.

On a personal level, senior managers constantly wrestled with the dilemma of whether change was moving at the right pace. If employees felt overwhelmed or the consultant thought the process was moving too slowly, they often questioned management's judgment and leadership. During these periods, senior managers feel frustrated, isolated, and alone, and face fears of failure if the change is not implemented effectively. Resolving these frustrations and dilemmas is a judgment call based on assessments, reactions, and intuition about the input being received, as well as personal observations. Thus, managing the speed of change requires intimate knowledge of when it can be accelerated and when it cannot, a long term view that balances the day-to-day operations with the strategic objectives, and the self-knowledge necessary to maintain one's convictions in the face of significant pressures.

What Does "Fast" Mean?

OD consultants, and the client systems that use them, need to be clear about what fast cycle time means. Data and experience suggest that there are at least three perspectives or dimensions to "fast cycle time strategic change:" what is requested, what is wanted, and what is acceptable.

What the Client Requests

The first aspect to determining what "fast" means is to recognize that what the client requests is not necessarily what they want or will be acceptable to them. It is fair to say that when clients ask for "fast cycle strategic change," they probably have some process and a desired end state in mind, and would like to reach that end state as quickly as possible. The client is asking for the whole thing, formulation and implementation of a major strategic reorientation, in six months. This is also what the consultant hears and believes the client wants.

What the Client Wants

The second aspect to what "fast" means is to examine what the client really wants when they say they need "fast cycle time strategic change." In our experience, what the client really wants is "painless" change. In the cases above, explicitly or implicitly, the clients understood that the organization needed to change in some major and substantive way, and they were under pressure to accomplish that objective quickly. Stress and pressure invoke psychological states that accentuate problems, pain, and difficulty. Hiring a consultant is a way to get expert help and may be seen as a way out of admitting that the client feels powerless. It is at this stage that tricky ethical situations arise.

Our fear is that in trying to be "customer oriented," too many OD practitioners ignore the realities of change implementation at best, or promise something they cannot deliver at worst. In trying to satisfy the customer, practitioners fall prey to agreeing with the client. Instead of clarifying what the client wants or will be satisfied with, the consultant consciously or unconsciously cooperates with the client rather than facing rejection. In reality, the client may be looking for the consultant to clearly define the possibilities or constraints; getting straight information is a perfectly good reason to ask for consulting assistance. Practitioners must be aware of their own motivations and be willing to help the client clearly define their motivations and expectations, or the possibility for an ethical conflict exists.

The other side of the ethical coin is that clients are uncertain or unaware of what they want and what they will accept. Practitioners and researchers have delivered important methodologies, such as large-group conferencing, for completing various phases of strategic change quickly. However, managers often balk at using these technologies. Bringing hundreds of people into a room, especially if it includes customers, regulators, and other external stakeholders, may be intimidating. Change itself is risky and the thought of using a "new" technology to bring about something risky often threatens a manager's sense of control. Defensive routines, such as "I don't want our dirty laundry aired in public," are common.

In sum, if the OD practitioner and the client are unclear about what they want from a fast cycle change process, the possibility for an ethical dilemma is quite real. OD practitioners must be confident enough in their methods, their processes, and themselves to tell the client that accomplishing risky goals often requires risky methods.

What the Client Will Accept

The third aspect of understanding what "fast" is requires defining what is an acceptable amount of change in a short time frame. Both cases suggest that "fast" means that the key ideas of the new strategic orientation are formulated quickly, or that there is a clear sense of how the change will be accomplished, and how long it will take. It may also include decisions about resources, and the key initial steps to set the organization on a new course. Although the managers we have worked with agree that they typically wanted everything implemented yesterday, they were satisfied with, "just get the ship pointed in the right direction quickly."

Thus, an important caution for OD practitioners is to be careful about the commitments made and the labels used to describe the change. By definition, change requires time, and labels like "transformational change" or "fast cycle" suggest that speed exists in places where it might not. If by change one restricts its meaning to the key ideas and concepts that define some future state, as in a "change in our thinking," then these labels make sense. But if these terms imply not only the formulation of new strategic orientations but their implementation as well, then the labels are misleading. Large-scale change implementation is not likely to follow preprogrammed schedules of completion. Breakthrough technologies, such as the large-group conference, permit practitioners to help clients see new ideas and possibilities quickly. However, it is dangerous to believe that these possibilities can be implemented in the same time frame.

Practitioners must exercise caution and apply their knowledge of the change process in the contracting phase. We can contract with clients about what they mean by "change," what change they expect, and how quickly it can be accomplished. In our attempt to be seen as relevant and helpful, we have the responsibility to avoid unconsciously misleading our clients about what is and is not achievable.

Effectiveness as a Source of Speed

The organization learning approach suggests that an important source of cycle time reduction is the knowledge embedded in the organization about how to change. Organizations that have successfully implemented change in the past have knowledge available to them about what worked and what did not work. Unfortunately, the knowledge gained today that will be useful in managing change in the future is not often cultivated or valued by the organization. Under the pressures to produce goods and services faster, cheaper, and of higher quality, developing knowledge about change management is a luxury that most organizations do not believe they can afford. Their hesitancy is understandable; a strategic change management capability is a latent one that is not used every day, or even every year, and maintaining that capability has a cost. Thus, despite the competitive advantage that might result from nurturing the capabilities to diagnose strategic orientations, formulate new strategies, and design and implement change agendas quickly, organizations do not allocate resources to developing a change management capability. (Interestingly, this is exactly what the big consulting firms are doing and what many organizations are buying.)

This short-term reality, however, hides a longer-term imperative. Only organizations that can sustain their performance, and have the inherent capability to accelerate the change process, are able to compete in environments demanding change and responsiveness. This suggests the utility of slack resources. Effective organizations are able to generate slack resources (i.e., profits and learnings) and then focus them on change. Ineffective organizations do not have the resources—either because they do not generate profits or because they have not embedded the learnings from past changes—to execute the complex activities associated with strategic change. When the capability to change is needed, organizations that have sustained their performance at such levels to nurture a strategic change capability are better equipped to change quickly.

SUMMARY

There are several important ways to decrease the amount of time required to formulate and implement substantive change in organizations. The opportunities for reducing cycle time in strategic analysis, strategy making, and designing a strategic change agenda are greater than the opportunities for speed in implementation. By recognizing what can and cannot be accelerated, understanding that managers often request more than they will accept, and by working with organizations to build competencies to change, OD practitioners can help organizations change more easily and quickly and sustain high levels of performance.

SUGGESTED READINGS

Argyris, C., & Schon, D. (1996). *Organization learning II* (2d ed.). Reading, MA: Addison-Wesley.

Beckhard, R., & Harris, R. (1987). *Organizational transitions: Managing complex change* (2d ed.). Reading, MA: Addison-Wesley.

Bourgeois, III, L. (1981). On the measurement of organizational slack. *Academy of Management Review, 6*(1): 29–39.

Cummings, T., & Worley, C. (1997). *Organization development and change* (6th ed.). St. Paul, MN: West Publishing Co.

Cummings, T., & Mohrman, S. (1988). Self-designing organizations. In R. Woodman & W. Pasmore (Eds.), *Research on organization change and development*, vol. 2. Greenwich, CT: JAI Press.

Fombrun, C. (1992). *Turning points*. New York: McGraw-Hill.

Galbraith, J., & Kazanjian, R. (1986). *Strategy implementation: Structure, systems and process* (2d ed.). St. Paul, MN: West Publishing Co.

Greiner, L., & Bhambri, A. (1989). New CEO intervention and the dynamics of deliberate strategic change. *Strategic Management Journal, 10*: 67–86.

Hamel, G., & Prahalad, C. (1995). *Competing for the future*. Cambridge, MA: Harvard University Press.

Hrebiniak, L., & Joyce, W. (1984). *Implementing strategy*. New York: Macmillan Publishing.

Ketchen, D., et al. (1997). Organizational configurations and performance: A meta-analysis. *Academy of Management Journal, 40*(1): 222–240.

March, J. (1981). Footnotes on organizational change. *Administrative Science Quarterly, 26*: 563–597.

Meyer, C. (1996). *Fast cycle time*. New York: The Free Press.

Robert, M. (1993). *Strategy pure and simple*. New York: McGraw-Hill.

Miller, D., & Friesen, P. (1980). Momentum and revolution in organizational adaptation. *Academy of Management Journal, 23*(4): 591–614.

Pettigrew, A., (1985). *The awakening giant: Continuity and change at ICI*. New York: Basil Blackwood.

Rumelt, R. (1974). *Strategy, structure and economic performance*. Boston: Harvard University Press.

Senge, P. (1990). *The fifth discipline*. New York: Doubleday.

Sorensen, P., Head, T., Scoggins, H., & Larsen, H. (1990). The turnaround of Scandinavian Airlines: An OD perspective. *Organization Development Journal*, Spring: 1–5.

Thompson, A., & Strickland, A. (1996). *Strategic management* (7th ed.). Homewood, IL: BPI/Irwin.

Tushman, M., & Romanelli, E. (1985). Organizational evolution: A metamorphosis model of convergence and reorientation. In L. Cummings & B. Staw (Eds.), *Research in organization behavior*, vol. 7. Greenwich, CT: JAI Press, 171–222.

Worley, C., Hitchin, D., & Ross, W. (1996). *Integrated strategic change*. Reading, MA: Addison-Wesley.

PART II

Change Directed at the Organizational Level

Search Conferencing: Accelerating Large-Scale Strategic Planning

Ronald E. Purser, Steve Cabana,
Merrelyn Emery, and Fred Emery

INTRODUCTION

Business organizations effect large-scale strategic change to increase their success in seizing business opportunities and countering competitive threats. One of the greatest challenges that business leaders face is quickly engaging all employees to plan and execute strategic change. Moreover, the traditional "top-down" process of strategic planning has proved to be too slow and cumbersome in these fast-paced times. Indeed, the speed and unpredictability of change in global markets renders charting any strategic path to be fraught with uncertainty. Road maps can no longer be relied upon. The global business terrain shifts indecently.

Planning large-scale strategic change for innovation, growth, or renewal entails moving organizations into uncharted territory. As managers venture to lead organizations into these uncharted territories, existing maps of business terrains are of little use. A sketch map of the business terrain is often the best that is available. Successful organizations will be those that learn how to quickly maneuver in shifting terrains, rather than relying on maps based on their historical success.

This process of creative organizational change falls outside the domain of traditional rational planning. Planning for a future state that is unknown requires a different type of organizational compass—one that helps organizations to respond

31

proactively to environmental discontinuities and shifting circumstances. *Discontinuities* are unpredictable events that preclude the use of rational forecasting planning methods. Such discontinuities might have their genesis in technological innovation, shifts in consumer attitudes or social values, changes in government regulations, or new and unconventional competitors.

Conventional approaches to planning are also not effective in facilitating cooperation and commitment across boundaries in large bureaucratic organizations. Instead, conventional planning processes treat planning as a task that can be divided up into bits and pieces. As intelligence gathering is assigned to different staff and functional specialists, other diagnostic activities are outsourced to consultants, while an elite group at the top of an organization acts as the brain of the firm. The plan then has to be rolled out to the rest of the organization, and numerous meetings are held in each functional area and at different levels of the management hierarchy. Implementation only gets underway after there is sufficient "buy in" to senior management's plan. Many well-laid plans like this have either been filed away in a drawer, or their implementation has floundered. Why? One reason is that conventional planning methods segment thinking from doing and planning from implementation. By contrast, mobilizing large-scale strategic change requires the creativity and commitment of all people throughout organizations and communities. In turbulent business and market environments, every employee must take responsibility for the future of the enterprise.

This top-down, cascade approach to planning is becoming less viable in a world of discontinuities. Despite this, many executives and managers still continue to concede to planning processes suited to a stable environment that is long gone. In today's uncertain environment, it is important that managers recognize that their enterprise must learn and plan as an open system if it is to survive. In an open system enterprise, members need to function as a learning-planning community, one that is fully capable of continuously formulating and implementing new strategies that are responsive to changing demands. The search conference is a tool for building this organizational capacity for active adaptation.

A number of progressive and forward-thinking managers at Microsoft, Hewlett-Packard, Motorola, and Xerox found conventional approaches to planning were inadequate to the task of strategic organizational renewal. They discovered the search conference to be a new approach to planned change which involves employees directly in the process—not as a means of soliciting their input or getting their "buy in" to a master plan already crafted by those at the top or "enrolling" people in a vision, but to actually create and implement action-based strategies.

Search conferences have been used in a wide variety of organizations as an alternative approach to traditional corporate strategic planning meetings. Other utilities of the method include: kicking-off organizational renewal efforts; mergers of companies and hospitals; planning the future of cities, regions, industries, and professional associations; managing conflict between contentious parties and diverse interests groups; forging long-term partnerships with customers, suppliers or government regulators; and the development of system-wide plans for reinventing government.

This chapter examines several important dimensions of the search conference theory and method, showing why this large-group intervention methodology is particularly appropriate for planning in turbulent environments. A case study of Xerox's use of the search conference for organizational renewal illustrates the structure and dynamics involved in this large-group method. Finally, this chapter distinguishes features of the search conference from traditional organization development methods and other large group interventions in the field.

WHAT IS A SEARCH CONFERENCE?

The *search conference* is a participative approach to planning in real time that helps organizations to develop the capacity for active adaptation to turbulent environments. Organizations are successful in turbulent environments when employees at all levels are actively involved in learning and planning as a means to stay abreast of, and responsive to, changing environmental demands. The first search conference was held in 1960 to help with the merger of Bristol-Siddeley, two British aircraft engine makers. Known as the Barford Conference, this pioneering planning method was the ingenious invention of Fred Emery and Eric Trist. Trist and Emery observed that one of the key features of the conference was "that of *the great psychological intensity . . .* which was due to the *very high level of personal involvement in the overriding demand for intellectual integrity*" (Trist & Emery, 1960). Indeed, Emery and Trist had discovered how a systems approach to planning coupled with democratic, task-oriented work groups could be a powerfully motivating force for effecting strategic change. They also learned that a conference designed along democratic lines made external stimuli such as guest speakers, audio-visual aids, or training exercises completely unnecessary. A very considerable body of knowledge and experience has accumulated since their pioneering work in 1960, thus enabling more precise specification of the design requirements and deeper theoretical understanding of the dynamics of search conferences.

The search conference is normally a two-and-a-half-day event, which is usually held off-site in a retreat setting. Ideally, twenty to forty people are selected to participate in a search conference based on such criteria as their knowledge of the system, whether they offer a diverse perspective relative to the strategic issue under consideration, as well as their potential for taking responsibility for implementation. In this respect, participants attend not as representatives of stakeholder groups, but because of their importance to the conference task. The idea is to "get the *right* system in the room," those people who are critical to achieving the purpose of the search conference. Precise specification of the purpose of a search conference is crucial, for it determines how the conference system is defined, which, in turn, shapes the criteria for participant selection.

Participants in a search conference work on planning tasks in a mixture of large-group plenary sessions and small groups. As a whole community, participants scan their external environment, review their history, analyze the strengths and weaknesses of their current system, which provide a shared context for their most important tasks: the development of strategic goals and action plans. Strategic issues relevant to a system are debated and discussed by the entire conference community, while areas of agreement and common ground are mapped out through a process of generating, analyzing, and synthesizing data into an integrated community product. As the learning and planning for the achievement of shared purposes are an integral part of an evolving process, the specific outcomes of the search conference are open-ended and cannot be predicted in advance. If designed and managed properly, the learning process of a search conference can have a catalytic influence on people, helping them to move toward a shared future direction.

THEORETICAL UNDERPINNINGS OF THE SEARCH CONFERENCE

In organization development, OD practitioners need a practice theory to guide their actions, and Lewin's famous phrase, "there is nothing so practical as a good theory," still holds true. However, good theories have increasingly given way to a fascination with packaged techniques. This trend is due in part to competing market forces among consultants as they seek to differentiate their interventions, products, and methods. What has emerged in the field of organization development is a norm of methodological relativism, and an eclectic attitude among practitioners that anything goes—where technique has precedence over theory. The simplification of the systems concept of "equifinality" has been invoked as a sort of professional courtesy to support the idea that any approach can get good results. However, equifinality does not mean that "anything goes," or that "there are more ways to skin a cat." Equifinality refers to the property of open systems with their capacity to develop from one steady state to another by a variety of means. Different methods do not magically lead to the same results, especially if they are informed by different theories.

When a method is lacking a well-developed theory and conceptual knowledge base, it is a likely candidate for a fad. While it is not presumed here that there is "one best way" to design and manage search conferences, it is important to understand the behavioral science knowledge and theoretical underpinnings of the method as a prerequisite for informed practice. The search conference is not a tool or technique so much as it is a theory that is put into practice. The key theoretical principles that inform the design and management of search conferences are briefly explained below.

OPEN SYSTEMS THINKING

Based on an open systems view of organization, the search conference is designed to facilitate learning how to plan and adapt strategies in an environment of increasing turbulence and uncertainty. The evolution of the environment to a condition of turbulence—where the ground-rules of business shift in unpredictable ways—necessitates a systems approach to planning. Indeed, system thinking provides the underlying conceptual framework for search conference design. Systems display properties where the whole is often greater than the sum of its parts, which means that we cannot understand a system simply to be the summation or aggregate of its parts. Similarly, because organizations are systems, they must be viewed as wholes that are composed of parts or subsystems. Yet systems are not to be understood merely by recognizing interrelations, interdependencies, and dynamics between parts. Every organization also has an overriding "system principle" that serves to organize and govern different parts and subsystems into a functional whole.

As living systems, organizations must remain open and responsive to their environment if they are to maintain their coherence and survival. A well-functioning open system has the capacity for active adaptation; that is, a continuous organizational learning and planning capability. Open systems are constantly engaged in learning from the environment and adapting plans in response to what they learn. As Figure 3.1 illustrates, the design of a search conference consists of three phases organized into a task sequence that follows the logic of an open systems approach to learning and planning.

During the first phase, participants are engaged in learning about changes in their environment. The unit of analysis in a search conference is system-environment relations that determine survival. Conducting a broad and sweeping scan of their environment, conference participants pool their perceptions of significant changes, emerging trends, and likely future demands that results in a shared picture and appreciation of their system in its environment. Together they learn how their system is situated in a population of other systems that constitute an *extended social field.*

FIGURE 3.1 *The Open System Translated into the Search Conference*

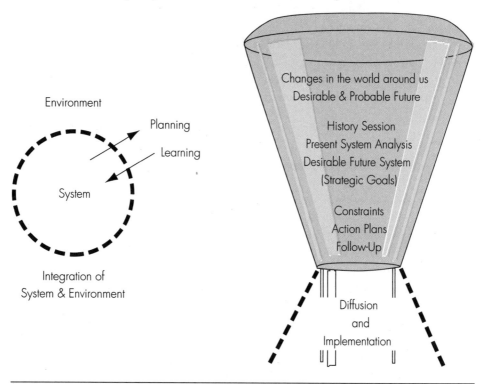

Furthermore, the tasks during this phase simultaneously work to build a community and unfreeze the system out of its complacency. Dissatisfaction with the status quo builds as participants learn about the environmental demands on their system and the need to respond more effectively to such demands in the probable future. During the second phase, the focus of the conference shifts to examining the system's internal capabilities. Participants focus attention on the past, present, and future of their system. This phase culminates in the generation of a shared vision based on participants' ideals for a more desirable future. The intent is to develop long-term strategies that enhance the system's capacity to respond to changing environmental demands. In the final phase, conference participants work on the development of practical next steps, action plans and strategies for overcoming system constraints.

The search conference is designed to develop a common database related to environmental trends and the need for change, a shared vision for a desirable future of the system, and clear next steps for moving the organization toward the desired future state. Beyond this, action groups will evolve strategies for the diffusion of the planned change process to others in the system. The change readiness formula developed by Gleicher, and popularized by Beckhard and Harris (1977),

$$C = abd > R,$$

where

C = Change,

a = Level of dissatisfaction with the status quo,

b = Desired future state,

d = Practical first steps toward desired state, and

R = costs of changing or resistance,

is reflected in the tasks performed within each phase of the conference. Through this interactive learning and planning process, the search conference develops the organizational capacity for large-scale strategic change.

Organizations are also purposeful and need to be organized so as to maximize the probability that the people within them can make the best choices regarding the means and ends that are critical to the survival of the enterprise. People in organizations need to be treated as purposeful human beings by giving them the freedom to choose and to act in the best interest of the whole. To actively adapt to turbulent environments, organizations are finding that they must draw upon the unused capabilities of their members, which requires more flexible and democratic structures.

For people to make conscious choices in the best interests of the whole, planning processes must elicit human ideals. Human systems, under the right social conditions, can become ideal seeking. Ideals represent shared aspirations around mutually acceptable ends and goals that constitute the common ground for cooperation and coordinated action. The democratic design philosophy, future focus, and open conditions for communications are deliberate attempts to create a social atmosphere conducive to the creative expression of human ideals.

An open system—whether it is a corporation, university, public agency or community—is also defined by a shared purpose, mission, core process, or primary task. Defining this shared purpose is critical to understanding the boundaries that demarcate the system from its environment. Similarly, a search conference creates a temporary organization that brings together a large group of people to plan the future of a system. One of the first steps involved in designing a search conference is to define the purpose or conference task. There must be some compelling business reason or challenging issue for convening a search conference, and the nature of this task will define the system that is to participate in the conference event.

DEMOCRATIC DESIGN PHILOSOPHY AND SELF-MANAGEMENT

The search conference is a temporary organization that locates responsibility for the coordination, control, and implementation of planning tasks in self-managing work groups. The conference structure creates a symmetrical dependency between managers and employees, forming multifunctional groups that have total responsibility for controlling and coordinating their own affairs to achieve mutually agreed to objectives. There is no hand-off or division of labor between thinkers and doers. Instead, the self-regulating work group constitutes the basic building block of organization, where control and redundancy are achieved by increasing the adaptiveness of individual members and enhancing the conditions for collaboration. This system principle is based on a democratic design philosophy known among theorists as the second organization design principle, or more simply, Design Principle 2 (DP2).

This is in stark contrast to the first design principle (DP1) with which we are familiar: bureaucratic organization. With the bureaucratic design philosophy, adaptiveness is achieved through elaborate social-control mechanisms and by designing in redundant and easily replaceable parts, so if one part fails, another can take over. This design philosophy may have sufficed when the costs of individual parts (labor) were low and the environment was relatively stable. The inherent message of a bureaucratic design philosophy is *you* do not count, *you* can easily be replaced, and *you* are expendable. Although bureaucratic structures were successful and viable during this time, the system itself was disempowering as people's psychological requirements for meaningful and productive work were not met. Treated like cogs in a machine, widespread worker alienation, discontent, and dependency have been the result. The logic of DP1, however, has not been limited to the dehumanization of labor on the shop floor; it also pervades top management echelons as planning is bureaucratized and fragmented into a separate activity divvied up to various experts and staff specialists. Similarly, we can see this design philosophy in educational institutions that operate like "knowledge factories," where masses of students are efficiently processed through the system. Likewise, in the traditional academic "talking heads" conference, responsibility for the content is invested in chairpersons, keynote speakers, experts, lecturers, those presenting papers, and so forth. In such traditional conferences, the audience—like employees in traditional organizations—are relegated to a passive role, devoid of responsibility, influence, and autonomy.

CREATIVE WORKING MODE

Through a democratic structure and clearly specified, time-bound tasks, the search conference establishes a "creative working mode." This mode occurs when a group is fully responsible for the control and coordination of their own work, with prior agreements established among members with regards to their overall purpose. The creative working mode is observed and operating when groups display high levels of energy, learning, cooperation, and sustained concentration towards completing tasks on time. It is akin to a condition that fosters group creativity. The theoretical basis for this is derived from Wilfred Bion's famous work on group dynamics. According to Bion, when people come together, they establish a group very quickly, and a group, like an individual, has a life of its own. A group is not just a collection of individuals, but a separate entity that has its own dynamics and behaviors, and operates according to certain assumptions. Bion observed that at any given time, a group is operating out of either a *work* or *basic assumption* mode.

When groups feel threatened and insecure, they fall prey to basic emotional assumptions as a means of preserving their group identity. Emotions become extraordinarily intensified, while intellectual abilities become markedly reduced. Bion is well known for his identification of three basic group assumptions: dependency, fight/flight, and pairing. When a group is in a dependency mode, members look to a leader to sustain the functioning of their group. This occurs in a bureaucratic structure in which individuals do not develop creative relationships with each other but instead depend upon a supervisor to tell them what to do. The emotional tone of a group is negative when basic assumptions are operating, and energy and learning are particularly low in a dependent group. In the grip of dependency, the learning process appears quite similar to the process of television viewing—people are passive, uncritical, and mentally lazy. In fight/flight, the official leader or expert is seen as inimical to the preservation of the group; members feel that they must either fight or flee. When group members are in a fight mode, their concern is with winning their arguments and making "telling points," not with mutual understanding. In flight, a group may unconsciously ignore directives and appear impatient, edgy, and distracted. "Pairing" can actually be a prelude to the creative working mode. Bion observed pairing when animated discussions between several members take precedence in a group that serves to divert attention towards some new hopeful idea. In this case, the pair is attempting to give birth to a new idea, yet the new idea remains unborn. With pairing, there is often a lot of hopeful talk, but little action or commitment.

The democratic, self-managing structure of the search conference works to minimize the outbreaks of group assumptions. Self-managing work groups are protected from outside interference and bureaucratic constraints, allowing them to channel their energy toward constructive ends. The search conference facilitator has the skills to manage these dynamics should they occur by redirecting the conference back into a work mode.

DIRECT PERCEPTION AND ECOLOGICAL LEARNING

The theory of ecological direct perception maintains that people have an innate ability to directly perceive meaning from the environment. Executives have long recognized the importance of direct perception, of having a firm grasp of business realities rather than relying upon secondhand data. Bill Gates, for example, meets regularly with the CEOs of all the major hardware and software firms, enabling him to spot trends and anticipate new developments. Since the environment contains an abundance of richly detailed information, search conferences are designed to restore confidence in people to trust their own perceptions and to develop local theories of their situation. This methodology assumes that any person with an intact perceptual system can directly access relevant information about the organization and environment. Only habit, a lack of confidence, or physical isolation prevents people from having access to information in the environment. Bureaucratic organizations, however, are notorious for segmenting those who have traditionally held responsibility for thinking and planning from those who are expected to obediently follow and implement the plans handed down from on high. Social stratification is inevitable in tall and dominant hierarchies. The masses of people employed in bureaucratic organizations are losing confidence in their own perceptions as they become more dependent upon experts and staff specialists to solve organizational problems.

Critical knowledge for active adaptive planning in any enterprise is not in the heads of a few specialists or executives. It is widely distributed among all employees. Experts can be helpful, but in search conferences they play a supporting role. Furthermore, high commitment is earned through participative planning, not analytical detachment. Participants in a search conference temporarily set aside their spreadsheets in order to search for possibilities that may not be inherent in existing bodies of data and current notions of what is relevant to their future. The emphasis is on becoming more open and perceptive of trends and possibilities on the horizon.

CONDITIONS FOR EFFECTIVE COMMUNICATIONS

A search conference capitalizes on the rich potential of face-to-face human communication. This potential goes beyond the ordinary maxim for "improving communication." Rather, the search conference establishes the conditions for effective and influential communications by creating a shared context for collaborative group work. Communication has come to be equated as meaning simply an exchange of information between a sender and receiver. But this digitized conception of communication—now expressed in such phrases as "interact," "connect," "interface," "network"—convey a completely different tone from the richness of being engaged in real face-to-face conversations.

Establishing the conditions for effective communications is necessary in order to sustain a fully democratic dialogue among diverse people. And sustaining a fully democratic dialogue requires the development of trust between participants. This is an essential part of the search conference. Drawing from the work of social psychologist Solomon Asch, the search conference is designed to create and maintain the following conditions:

1. *Openness.* The conference is structured so that all information is shared openly and that things are what they appear to be. In other words, there is no master plan, hidden agendas, or secret deals going on behind the scenes—all information is available.
2. *Psychological similarity.* Official status differences are minimized by working within self-managing groups governed by a ground rule where all perceptions are allowed equal airtime. The sharing of perceptions related to past, present, and future of the enterprise, especially the focus on shared ideals, establishes the sense that participants at the conference are psychologically similar and share similar concerns.
3. *Mutually shared field.* Participants experience, through pooling their perceptions of their organization in its environment, a mutually shared objective field— a sense that they all live in the same world—a world that can make sense and is knowable.
4. *Trust.* The previous three conditions lead to a spiral of trust, allowing the formation of a fully functioning, learning-planning community that must be sustained by ensuring the continuity and development of its self-managing structure.

The first condition, "openness," is critical to all facets of search conference design and management. In operational terms, this means ensuring that participants can become oriented to the larger environmental context and its relevance in such a way that all knowledge is public. One important consequence of this is that disagreement about the outside world appears to be public disagreement about matters that are capable of communication and resolution. For this condition to be met, all data in a search conference is publicized and out in open view for inspection by all. Individual note-taking or filling out worksheets is discouraged in favor of recording perceptions on flip charts, while facilitators of the process refrain from becoming involved in the content of group discussions. Joint action is more likely to emerge when open communication allows participants to become aware of each other and their respective intentions, attitudes, and beliefs.

The second condition, "basic psychological similarity," amounts to a recognition that other people—despite their roles, position or status in the organization, or intelligence—are basically similar to ourselves in ways that distinguish us from non-humans. The search conference establishes a context in which people can observe others perceiving, feeling, and acting in ways similar to the way they perceive, feel, and act. More specifically, psychological similarity is established through the sharing of human ideals that are elicited when people articulate their vision and images for a more desirable future.

The search conference is also designed so that it leads to the emergence of what Asch called a "mutually shared field." As participants begin to see similar trends in the environment, they establish the presence of a field that has commonly perceived features. With the emergence of this shared context, people come to not only appreciate the common set of challenges facing their system, but they also develop greater appreciation of the unique challenges facing each individual. They also come to learn that their mutual interest in improving the effectiveness of their system is conditional on greater degrees of cooperation and coordination.

As these preceding conditions are established, the last condition for trust emerges and develops. Individual participants themselves begin to take on characteristics of open systems, adapting and changing their behavior in response to the actions of others within the system, and in correlation with changes in the environment.

RATIONALIZING CONFLICT

The rationalization of conflict is quite different from the consensus decision-making process. With consensus decision-making, parties that oppose an alternative are included in discussions but must eventually come around to support the decision. Edgar Schein operationally defines consensus as a psychological state induced through influential discussions such that "those members who would not take the majority alternative, nevertheless understand it clearly and are prepared to support it." This mode of decision-making can be very time consuming and frustrating when meetings are prolonged and extended with the hopes of reaching a consensus. Dissenting positions must be considered and talked through until everyone feels that they have had their say and are willing to go along with the majority consensus. With consensus decision-making, one or two issues that are in conflict can consume all of a group's time and attention, draining away their energy for productive work. There is a distortion of the balance between the amount of common ground and conflict in such groups.

In contrast, the rationalization of conflict procedure puts matters into proper perspective; it allows all parties to perceive the true ratio of agreement to disagreement, which in most cases is usually on the order of 85%:15%. For example, participants in a search conference will generate a list of multiple strategic goals. In some conferences, this list can contain ten to fifteen items. Out of these ten to fifteen items, usually only two to three of the items will be the objects of serious disagreements. The search conference facilitator helps the group sort out these items, distinguishing whether their points of contention are over semantics on how an item is phrased or worded, or whether it is rooted in substantive differences of opinion and logic. Items that provoke substantive disagreements are placed on a "disagree list." Once items in conflict are seen in proportion to the other items for which there is widespread agreement, the energy devoted to pursuing the few items in conflict dissipates. Since there are usually more items for which there is agreement, conference participants are usually quite eager to proceed forward on those, while leaving the contentious items on the disagree list.

USING THE SEARCH CONFERENCE
AT XEROX'S CUSTOMER BUSINESS UNIT

Xerox is facing pressures that all information technology companies are facing: worldwide competition, continually changing customer requirements, and rapidly changing technology. Prior to a recent reorganization, the largest business division within Xerox—United States Customer Operations—was comprised of sixty-five districts. This division was functionally organized with a centralized R&D unit, while engineering and manufacturing functions were responsible for producing products, and the operating company was responsible for sales. In this matrix structure, the product development process was slow and cumbersome, unable to keep up with environmental and customer demands. This resulted in a major reorganization of the division into thirty seven Customer Business Units (CBUs).

After the reorganization, each CBU had total responsibility for revenues, profits and customer satisfaction. CBUs were expected to become more entrepreneurial, and general managers were given wide latitude to run their own organizations. Under the old, centralized system, corporate headquarters provided fixed targets for revenue, profit, profit growth, market share, and customer satisfaction. Under the new decentralized system, CBUs would have to function in a more creative and flexible manner in order to improve customer satisfaction while lowering operating costs.

In 1995, the largest CBU in Xerox was formed when three separate Chicago area sales and service districts were consolidated. Due to downsizing, the morale in this unit was low, while many of the departments were working at cross-purposes with each other. A recent employee opinion survey revealed that a shared mission for the CBU was severely lacking. These conditions provided the impetus for Dan Dotin, the vice president of the Illinois CBU, to seek a comprehensive approach that would bring about a large-scale change in the organization. To address this need, Ronald Purser, one of the authors of this chapter, was invited to consult with Dan Dotin and his manager of human resources, Chet Terry. After a brief educational introduction to the search conference method, Dotin and Terry quickly understood the utility of the search conference as a large-group intervention for effecting strategic alignment and organizational renewal. Their intent was to use the search conference as a means for aligning managers and employees from different functional areas towards a common strategic direction for the newly formed business unit. Dan Dotin recollects his challenges:

> Xerox had its first major restructuring of field operations. It was top-down downsizing. People were reeling and we had to find a way to get them reconnected in a new organization. I didn't want to work through the layers of management. I wanted leaders to emerge and faster decisions to be made. That meant bringing managers and employees together

around a common set of strategic goals. I chose a search conference as the planning method to make that happen. Our task was to form strategies that would earn our customers' loyalty. It had to be a strategy worthy of being deployed. We discovered that a search conference speeds up the planning cycle so we can act quickly to start implementing the plan. It works because it plants the seeds of diffusion into the strategic plan.

To prepare Xerox's management for the search conference, the consultant, Ronald Purser, met with Dan Dotin's top management team to provide additional education on the search conference process and its theoretical underpinnings. This was also an occasion to test for their level of commitment and support. After a spirited question and answer session, the management team was supportive of trying a new approach to planning that would involve fifty people from different functions and levels within the organization. Purser worked with the management team to formulate the stated purpose of the search conference. Defining the purpose of the conference is one of the most important tasks, for it specifies why the conference is being convened and what the expected outcomes for the events are. The management team was also made aware that one of their responsibilities was to communicate and explain to their employees the purpose of the conference. Subsequent meetings with the management team were convened for deciding upon criteria relevant to selecting employees and managers who would be invited to participate in the search conference. As in all search conferences, the people selected should be those who have critical knowledge of the organization and environment and can take responsibility for implementing the plan. One key question to ask in selecting participants will be "Can this person actively contribute to achieving the stated purpose of the search conference?" The consultant's task is to help the planning group wrestle with these questions and prepare the organization for the intervention.

The stated purpose of the Xerox search conference was "To develop a shared future direction for the achievement of a market driven CBU in the next twenty-four to thirty-six months." A stratified sample of positions from each department and level within the CBU was used to identify fifty participant slots. Then managers from different functions made recommendations as to people who could potentially fill their slots, and nominations from employees were also sought. Fifty percent of the participants were selected from the management staff, while the other half were drawn from lower and middle levels of the organization. In preparation for the conference, Dan Dotin and Chet Terry held numerous informational meetings with employees to communicate the purpose for the conference, explaining the need for developing a long-range strategy for the business, and to further educate employees on the search conference process.

The Xerox search conference was designed as a three-day event, beginning with introductions, expectation setting, and a scan of the environment towards late afternoon of the first day. The session was held offsite at a nearby hotel and participants were encouraged to stay overnight to create social island conditions. Participants worked on tasks alternating between large group plenary sessions and small self-managing groups. Using this format, the conference began with a large-group brainstorming session where participants identified key trends and forces within the social environment and their industry. This environmental analysis is critical to every search conference as it provides a shared context in which planning can occur. In a very short period, the search conference develops a common database about changes in the world, market demands, customers' needs, industry trends, technological changes, and corporate pressures—a collective map of the system in its environment. This collective map of the Xerox environment was posted across an entire wall in front of the conference room. Small groups were then instructed to analyze the implications of what these trends mean for the future of the CBU. The key question to be addressed was: "What is the likely probable future environment for the CBU if it does nothing and continues to operate in a business-as-usual manner?" Their collective assessments revealed compelling reasons for the need for change:

There will be a loss of market share, more customer pressure, and a decrease in customer satisfaction.

The role of the CBU, within Xerox, will diminish both in terms of personnel and responsibility.

CBU revenues will decrease and will continue to lose market share and people. There will be a rapid increase in alternative distribution channels.

There will be a depersonalized work environment; technology will provide the opportunity to market intellectual capital, but our size will prohibit the rapid reaction critical to survival.

The next day the conference shifted to generating relevant diagnostic data about the internal functioning of the organization. This also included a historical appreciation of their organization as participants identified the cultural aspects and traditions that they want to preserve and carry forward into the future. Tables were pushed aside and fifty chairs were rearranged in a large circle in preparation for the history session. As the focus was on the past, it was a time for participants to revisit their core values, early work culture, developmental milestones, crisis points, and achievements. Those who had the longest tenure in the company, the elders, were asked first to speak. Looking back, many of the senior people recollected the challenges and strengths that characterized the Xerox culture:

A lot of people think our jobs were easy back then, but I can tell you, we had to make cold calls. Customers had to be sold on the concept of photocopying. They didn't know what a Xerox machine was . . .

I think one of our biggest strengths is that we have always been able to figure out a way to get things done. When we were just starting out, we had to invent and make up procedures as we went along. While we have standardized many of our processes to improve quality, I think we need to revisit and revitalize the entrepreneurial spirit in the company . . .

I am a technician and I can remember when the sales agent used to take me with him on sales calls. That is unheard of today. Because we all knew each other from this cross-fertilization, you knew who to call if you had a problem . . .

We developed strong bonds with people at work from socializing outside the office. We have lost this aspect of our culture. We need to recapture this connection to people. Today we only communicate with each other through voice mail or E-mail. It's not enough . . .

The retelling of significant historical events, reminiscing about the details of significant turning points and their relation to how the company has evolved over time, reaffirmed the strengths of the Xerox culture and established a sense of belongingness and community. Asch's conditions for psychological similarity were enhanced during the history session as participants began to appreciate the human dimensions of change and development of the organization through time. The large-circle seating arrangement during this session also contributed to a feeling of equality, since participants could choose to tell their story without regard for their status or position.

Once participants had developed a shared appreciation of their organization's challenges and past strengths, they were ready to analyze the functioning of their current sociotechnical system. By this point in the conference, participants had discovered some areas of common ground, and a sufficient level of trust had developed, allowing them to honestly confront aspects of their current system that are working well and that need to be maintained, problematic areas or outmoded procedures that need to be changed or discontinued, as well as processes that currently do not exist but that need to be created. This diagnosis of the present system generated useful data and creative ideas for change.

By the evening of the second day, small groups worked to develop a shared vision that described the desirable future state of the Xerox CBU system three years out. The output of all the previous tasks became inputs for this task; participants were advised to set existing constraints aside and to exercise their creativity and imagination, and dream large. The search conference followed Lippit's research that found groups that focus their attention on their preferred future are more likely to exhibit positive energy, commitment, and enthusiasm compared to those that get mired in solving past or present problems. However, the goal is not so much trying to predict the future but to elicit peoples' ideals for the type of future they wish to create. By definition, a desirable future is based on ideals; it cannot be fully realized or attained. Envisioning the desired future state is also very different from conventional planning techniques that simply extrapolate current trends into the future. Instead, participants in the search conference are engaged in ideal-seeking behavior, collectively imagining the type of future they are intrinsically motivated to help create, and then barn-raising their plans together as a learning community.

A lofty image of a desirable future for the system is backed up with a concrete and coherent set of strategic goals, long-range targets, and descriptions of desired end points. Specifying these long-term objectives provides a pragmatic basis for translating a desirable future into a clear set of action and implementation plans. Working in small groups, participants in the Xerox search conference generated a list of ten strategic goals. Then, in the plenary session, facilitators helped the large group to integrate and prioritize the list. This was done by merging items that were similar across small-group reports, separating unique and stand-alone items, and identifying conflicting items between different group reports. For goals in conflict, facilitators placed these items on the "disagree list." By the end of the evening, all fifty of the Xerox participants had come to publicly agree upon five key strategic objectives:

1. The CBU is market-driven and recognized as the vendor-of-choice in the local market.
2. Fully empowered employees who are accountable and have incentives to meet their customers' requirements, with the only boundary being ethical behavior.
3. An organizational design based on cross-functional work groups to increase profits by 15% and revenue growth by 20% per year.
4. Continuous bottom-up planning as the norm used by all employees and managers as a means for continuous learning and improvement.
5. Mastery of technology tools that fully support business needs throughout the organization.

The last phase of the search conference began on the third day, devoted entirely to action planning and deliberating on how implementation should proceed. Participants self-selected themselves into action-planning groups that coalesced around each of the five key strategic goal statements. Before plunging directly into implementation planning, these groups spent several hours developing specific strategies that outlined how existing and probable constraints to achieving their strategic objectives could be overcome. Constraints are challenging and difficult to deal with, which is why they are addressed towards the end of the search conference. Many conventional approaches to planning attempt to deal with constraints head-on. Converging upon constraints early in the conference would inhibit creative thinking, narrowing the focus to solving current problems, rather than opening up the search for fruitful and innovative possibilities for the future. Interim reports from each of the five action planning groups were taken before lunch.

After lunch, action-planning groups returned to develop action plans for each of the five strategic objectives by outlining some practical next steps and who needed to be involved, along with project milestones. For example, the action-planning group working on the implementation of cross-functional work teams reported:

1. Within three weeks, members of the team will engage the rest of CBU, communicating the intended strategies for redesign into a cross-functional team structure.
2. Within one month, members of the team will benchmark other companies.
3. Within three months, other key players and voluntary members will be recruited to assist with the planning and redesign effort. Action-team members will create a newsletter to keep all CBU employees informed of the redesign process.
4. Within four months, existing Quality Improvement Teams (QITs), whose composition is already made up of cross-functional members, will be utilized for collecting and analyzing data related to key issues in the CBU.
5. Within six months, a cross-functional team structure for the CBU will be defined.
6. A cross-functional team will be trained in the Participative Design methodology and pilot-tested by the end of the year.
7. By the first quarter of 1996, a transition plan for moving the entire CBU into cross-functional work teams will be in place.

Towards the end of the day, a plenary session was held in which participants discussed the next steps that needed to be taken following the conference. "We all agreed to have a progress review session forty-five days after the conference," noted one participant several months after the conference. Another critical element that came out of the follow-up session is that action teams agreed to organize numerous diffusion meetings throughout the organization after the conference. These diffusion meetings were used to communicate the results of the search conference and to involve more personnel in the development and implementation of action plans. This large-scale diffusion process eventually provided an opportunity for all managers and employees in the Xerox CBU to develop a shared understanding of their strategic goals and to become involved in some aspect of the implementation process.

After a search conference, participants have the ownership and momentum to take action plans forward. Effort must be made, however, to ensure the continuity of self-managing teams once they return to their organization. Organizational reentry of action-planning teams requires careful planning, ensuring that they have the authority and legitimacy to implement the plan. Action-planning teams need sanctioning from sponsors; they need access to resources, information, and time to meet. Parallel learning structures can be set up that allow action-planning teams to continue their work unimpeded by bureaucratic constraints. In addition, action-planning teams can establish "link-up groups" —other people in the organization that need to be either directly involved, informed, or consulted as the process of implementation unfolds. A search conference shows that while the commitment of top management is essential to the development of a plan, it is the commitment of the rest of the organization that translates the plan into action. Action-planning teams play a key role in mobilizing the whole organization around the large-scale change process and implementation.

A Brief Assessment

Six months after the search conference, Dan Dotin made this assessment of the most significant results achieved so far:

> We used the output from the search conference action-planning teams in our annual planning process to develop the business strategy for the next three years. Our culture has engineered a big shift. We've moved from being highly dependent on top-down planning to acting like entrepreneurs. This is an incredible breakthrough for our front-line employees. Each action-planning team and the associates they recruited devoted countless hours to integrate their output into the business plan. I put one of our top sales managers on special assignment to work full-time to integrate the work of all the action teams into our business practices. From a best practices point of view, the Xerox World-Wide Service group selected our CBU as one of two sites as a pilot for further work to improve customer loyalty because of the results we achieved with the search conference. We are now implementing the cross-functional design strategies that came out of the search conference so Xerox can organize around tasks rather than functions. I am excited about the next year as people carry the plan forward.

IMPLICATIONS AND FUTURE TRENDS

The search conference is a large group intervention designed for the purpose of building an intentional learning-planning community. In contrast, most organization development interventions were designed for improving group processes and solving problems at the small-group level. Teambuilding, process consultation, and action research have frequently been used for these purposes. The search conference departs from these more familiar methods in several respects. First, search conferences focus on the system level of organization, including up to forty participants from multiple levels and widely dispersed departments and functions. Teambuilding interventions are focused at the group, intergroup, or subunit levels mainly for improving within-group cohesion. Working within the boundaries of functional groups, teambuilding rarely addresses whole system and long-term strategic issues for improving organization-environment relations. Second, search conferences democratize the entire planned change process in that participants are in control of the data collection, diagnosis, feedback, and action planning activities. In contrast, action research interventions are typically more consultant-centered, as the consultant has responsibility for gathering relevant information through interviews or surveys, analyzing and diagnosing the data, and cascading the feedback of findings downwards to select groups. Third, search conferences do not focus on solving existing problems or finding the causes of past problems; rather, they are concerned with developing shared ideals and plans for creating a more desirable future for the organization. Traditional OD interventions are oriented towards diagnosing the underlying causes of presenting problems and existing symptoms. They often lack a big picture focus, failing to take into account the larger contextual environment. Moreover, a narrow focus on problem solving can drive out more innovative and creative solutions that often diverge from existing frameworks and assumptions.

The trend to include and involve more organizational members in large group meetings is gaining momentum. However, the search conference methodology differs from other large group interventions that have recently emerged in several important respects. First, the search conference was designed specifically to be used as a method for planning organizational or community futures, not for organizational design. Some methods (for example, Dick Axlerod's "Conference Model") have adapted search-like processes for the purpose of speeding up the sociotechnical redesign of organizations. Second, there is a cultural predilection in the United States to believe "bigger is better," as some practitioners (for example, Kathleen Dannemiller and Robert Jacob's "Large-Scale Technology") are now convening conferences with 150 to 500 participants. These large-group events might be useful for enhancing information sharing across functional boundaries. However, the quality, depth of dialogue, and solidity of joint agreements around long-term purposes is not equivalent to a group of thirty-five to forty participants, which is the upper limit in a search conference. Also, attempts to use the search conference for redesign purposes may evoke a great deal of resistance once the project transitions to the implementation stage. Even large group interventionists must still adhere to the famous axiom of "starting where the system is at." Search processes used for speeding up the sociotechnical systems analysis may actually confuse people as they are asked to become involved in a complex process that requires careful analysis and decision-making. Involving too many people, too fast, and taking on too much information is bound to lead to cognitive overload and other unforeseen problems. Other methods (for example, Marvin Weisbord and Sandra Janoff's "Future Search") that resemble a search conference have made significant alterations to the methodology such that they are more suited for "visioning" or consensus building but not strategic planning and community building. The search conference, on the other hand, aims for more than better information sharing across functional boundaries or consensus-building among diverse stakeholder groups. Rather, the intended result is to produce a committed group of knowledgeable people who have: a deep understanding of the challenges confronting their organization; a set of solid agreements about the ideals that the change and strategy are supposed to serve and action plans that are in alignment with these ideals; and a social mechanism for participation and diffusion process for engaging the whole system in the implementation of the planned change. This last point suggests a future trend of running multiple search conferences, either in parallel or contiguously. Microsoft Corporation has, for example, conducted a series of search conferences in their product development division, culminating in an integrative session to consolidate strategies and action plans.

In these turbulent times, people are losing faith in institutions, retreating from civic and community life, and becoming less willing and able to participate as citizens in the affairs central to the functioning of a democratic society. Organizations must strike a balance between satisfying the needs of individuals with the needs for building economically viable and effective organizations. For this to happen, planning in organizations must be done *by the people, for the people, and with the people.* The search conference is one medium for enabling people to take part fully in shaping the destiny of their organization and to make decisions for the common good.

SUGGESTED READINGS

Ackoff, R. (1994). *The democratic corporation.* New York: Oxford Books.

Argyris, C., Putnam, R., & Smith, D. (1985). *Action science.* San Francisco: Jossey-Bass.

Asch, S. (1952). *Social psychology.* Englewood Cliffs, NJ: Prentice Hall.

Beckhard, R., & Harris, R. (1977). *Organizational transitions: Managing complex change.* Reading, MA: Addison-Wesley.

Bion, A. (1961). *Experiences in groups and other papers.* London: Tavistock Publications.

Emery, F. E. (ed.). (1969). *Systems thinking,* vol.1. Harmondsworth, England: Penguin Books.

Emery, F. E. (1981). The emergence of ideal-seeking systems. In F. E. Emery (Ed.) *Systems Thinking,* vol. 2. Harmondsworth, England: Penguin Books.

Emery, M., & Purser, R. E. (1996). *The search conference: A powerful method for planning organizational change and community action.* San Francisco: Jossey-Bass.

Gibson, J. (1979). *The ecological approach to visual perception.* Boston: Houghton-Mifflin.

Mirvis, P. (1988). Organization development: Part I—an evolutionary perspective. In W. Pasmore & R. Woodman (Eds.), *Research in organizational change and development,* vol. 2. Greenwich, CN: JAI Press.

Schein, E. (1969). *Process consultation: Its role in organization development.* Reading, MA: Addison-Wesley.

Trist, E., & Emery, F. E. (1960). Report on the Barford Conference for Bristol/Siddeley Aero-Engine Corporation. Document no. 598, July, 1960. London: Tavistock.

ADDITIONAL READINGS RELATED TO SEARCH CONFERENCING

A more complete critique of traditional strategic planning can be found in Henry Mintzberg's *The Rise and Fall of Strategic Planning* (New York: The Free Press, 1994); in David Hurst's *Crisis and Renewal: Meeting The Challenge of Organizational Change* (Boston: HBS Press, 1995); and in his earlier article in *Organizational Dynamics,* "Why Strategic Management Is Bankrupt" (1986).

The most comprehensive book on the theory and practice of the search conference can be found in Merrelyn Emery and Ronald Purser's *The Search Conference: A Powerful Approach to Planning Organizational Change and Community Action* (San Francisco: Jossey Bass, 1996). A more historical and theoretical account of the method can be found in a monograph by Merrelyn Emery, *Searching: for New Directions, in New Ways, for New Times* (Canberra: Centre for Continuing Education, Australian National University, 1982). Another good treatment of the theory of planning in a turbulent environment using search conferences appeared in an overlooked book by Trevor Williams, *Learning to Manage Our Futures* (New York: Wiley, 1982). The emergence of the search conference method was recognized as part of the next wave in large-scale change by Fred Emery and Eric Trist's book *Toward a Social Ecology: Contextual Appreciation of the Future in the Present* (London: Tavistock, 1973). And the third volume of the Tavistock anthology, *The Social Engagement of Social Science* (Philadelphia: University of Pennsylvania Press, 1996), edited by Fred Emery and Beluah Trist, contains accounts of how and why search conferencing emerged as a methodology for large systems change within a socioecological paradigm. A number of interesting cases on the search conference method as it has been practiced in Canada can be found in *Learning Works: Searching for Organizational Futures* (Toronto: ABL Publications, 1989), edited by S. Wright and D. Morley.

A more in-depth account of the theory of active adaptation and the importance of ideals to planning can be found in Fred Emery's book *Futures We Are In,* (Leiden: Martinus Nijhoff, 1977). The search conference is based on systems thinking that is rooted in an understanding of contextualism. Steve Pepper's book *World Hypotheses* (Berkeley: University of California Press, 1942) provides a thorough explanation of contextualism. Some readers may be surprised to learn that systems thinking has been around for several decades, and Fred Emery's two volumes on *Systems Thinking* (London: Penguin Books, 1969;1981) are good sourcebooks. The reader may find a theoretical discussion of the conditions for influential, effective communication that inform the design of search conferences in Fred and Merrelyn Emery's book *A Choice of Futures* (Leiden: Martinus Nijhoff, 1976) as well as Solomon Ash's classic book *Social Psychology,* (Englewood Cliffs, NJ: Prentice Hall, 1952). Wilfred Bion's classic text *Experience in Groups* (London: Tavistock Publications, 1960) articulates how group assumption behavior differs from that of the conscious working mode. The democratic design principle, which is a central tenet of the search conference method, is derived from a long stream of action research in the redesign of industrial organizations. One can consult Fred Emery and Einar Thorsrud's *Democracy at Work* (Leiden: Martinus Nijhoff, 1976) or Merrelyn Emery's *Participative Design for Participative Democracy* (Canberra: Centre for Continuing Education, Australian National University, 1993), a more recent compendium of this movement towards more democratic structures in the workplace. Large-group interventions are becoming more popular, yet practice seems to be advancing faster than theory as Barbara Bunker and Billie Alban's special issue on large-group interventions in the December 1992 issue of the *Journal of Applied Behavioral Science* demonstrates. This issue contains an amalgam of articles that represent recent methodological developments in the field.

C H A P T E R 4

Accelerating Strategic Change at Amoco: Creating a Shared Services Organization

Merrill C. Anderson, Ph.D.

INTRODUCTION

The oil business has remained fundamentally unchanged for over 130 years: finding, acquiring, developing, producing, and distributing hydrocarbon assets. Swings in supply and demand have impacted product availability and pricing, which in turn has impacted the financial bottom lines of the oil companies. Since the late 1980s, supply has outstripped demand and oil prices have steadily dropped. This results in oil companies being ever vigilant in keeping costs low. The lower they keep their annual cost structure the less vulnerable they are to market swings.

One ripe target for aggressively managing cost has been with support service providers. Support functions like human resources, finance, information technology, and others have been under increasing pressure to reduce fixed costs. Human resource functions in North America, for example, have been reduced by 20% since 1985. Outsourcing and reengineering have been the primary tools to reduce support service costs.

One major challenge to reducing support service costs has been to not cripple the core work of the business in the process. Support services are typically entwined and deeply embedded in the core business. Cutting support services too deeply or with little understanding of the value these services provide to the core business could grind the business to a halt. Outsourcing does not *improve* the work, it merely shifts the work to an outside supplier. Reengineering holds promise to improve the work and reduce

55

overall cost, however, the embedded nature of the support work makes this approach problematic. Consequently, reengineering support work has tended to be more tactical in nature and focused on fixing smaller elements of larger support work processes.

In the late 1980s an entirely new approach to executing support work was undertaken: support work would be organized as a *shared service*. The intention of this shared service approach is to "separate the wheat from the chaff." All resources from a support service function would be pulled out from the core business and established as a separate entity. A shared service organization markets and sells its services to internal customers, realizes revenue, and is expected to cover all of its fully loaded costs by year-end. An internal marketplace is established to enable the exchange of goods and services. Internal market forces are then expected to appropriately shape the size and skill complement of the support group.

In 1994 Amoco Corporation based in Chicago, Illinois, embarked on a major restructuring. Its three operating companies were dismantled in favor of its seventeen business groups. These seventeen business groups then provided operational control for ninety-four business units. It was felt that removing the operating companies would reduce a layer of management and improve the speed of executing corporate business strategy.

This restructuring also created a new 6,300-person Shared Services organization consisting of fourteen support functions (e.g., Human Resources, Finance, Information Technology. and so on). Resources for this shared service organization were drawn from the three large operating companies as well as the corporate staff function. This reorganization represented a radical change, both in terms of the structure of the organization and in the way support services were delivered. These service organizations were now going to operate as cost centers, contracting for work with business group customers and formally charging for their services. Most Shared Services employees had to make the shift from being embedded in a business to formally selling their services to internal business customers in the new Amoco market place.

Amoco leadership felt that moving to a shared services concept would better position the seventeen business groups to manage—and reduce—support service costs. Once this decision was made, the issue was how to accelerate the shared service implementation as quickly as possible. This chapter describes how organization development methodology was created and utilized to accelerate the implementation of the shared service vision at Amoco.

THE SHARED SERVICES VISION

The vision of Shared Services was to become "a world class supplier, adding value through customer focus, cost leadership, and excellence." Part of the rationale for the Shared Services concept is to make cost drivers associated with support services visible and therefore easier to manage. In a largely commodity business, cost leadership can be a potent source of competitive advantage. The vision, however, also emphasizes customer focus and excellence.

There appeared to be two major challenges to successfully achieving this vision. One challenge was to find an appropriate balance among the three tenents of the vision for each of the fourteen Shared Service functions. For example, to what extent should Information Technology (IT) invest in technical excellence and develop a cadre of information systems consultants, recognizing that short-term service cost may go up as a result? Shared Services leaders needed to better understand how to shape the Shared Services organization to best serve the diverse needs of the seventeen business group customers, both in the short-term and the long-term. Too much emphasis on cost leadership could result in a failure to invest in skills needed for the future.

The second challenge was to explore the possibilities of generating even greater value by collaborating *across* functions. These functions had traditionally operated on their own. Amoco wanted to look for opportunities where collaboration among functions would demonstrate exceptional value to the business group customers. Customers had voiced concerns that overemphasizing investments, excellence, and value creation could require additional infrastructure and capital. These capital investments could eventually show up in the form of increased rates for services and threaten to put oil and gas commodity businesses in a less competitive cost position.

Successful implementation of the shared services concept was strategically critical for Amoco. While the broad outline of the organization was put into place and the fourteen functional groups established, the direction of how this organization would develop was not clear. The shared services vision offered three sets of choices—customer focus, cost leadership, and excellence—but little in the way of direction of how to make the choices.

ORGANIZING FOR CHANGE

A Shared Services Management Council (SSMC) was established that was comprised of the leaders for each of the fourteen shared services functions. These leaders were dedicated to design and develop their organizations in a way that would increase the cost competitiveness of the line businesses. A core team was created to coach SSMC leaders on how to accelerate implementation of the shared services concept. This core team consisted of internal change consultants and financial experts. External consultants were occasionally called upon for assistance.

The core team worked with the SSMC to broadly set the agenda for shared services implementation:

1. Operationally define the vision in terms of what the leaders could do in their respective functional organizations to implement the vision successfully;
2. Set direction for Shared Services to increase value creation for customers in a way that makes some choices about how to balance investment in functional excellence with cost leadership; and
3. Accelerate the evolution of the shared services concept to achieve competitive advantage.

The core team developed an innovative organization design methodology that held the promise of rapidly accelerating the evolution of shared services. In essence, this methodology was based on having the SSMC describe how they would like to see their organization evolve over time. Many generations over this evolutionary course would be described and discussed. All generations would be characterized and fleshed out. Then dialogue would turn to the possibility of skipping intermediary generations in order to realize the future-most generation sooner. In this way the implementation of shared services could be accelerated by many years.

AMOCO'S MULTIGENERATION ORGANIZATION DESIGN

Figure 4.1 illustrates how the multigeneration organization design methodology was adapted at Amoco to accelerate the evolution of Shared Services. There are four main steps in the process. The first step is to develop the conceptual framework for the process that includes characterizing the organization according to key attributes. The next step involves describing the organization according to these attributes and probing for themes or trends. The third step explores how to accelerate achieving the future state. The fourth and final step engages participants in committing to an action plan to achieve the business results they have identified.

Step One: Develop Framework

The first step in multigeneration organization design is to set the conceptual framework for the process. There is considerable preparation work with the organization's leadership that must take place. These initial discussions provided the data to define the set of organizational attributes. An *organizational attribute* is defined as an organization feature or activity that leaders can directly leverage to develop their respective organizations.

A consensus developed within the SSMC during the initial discussions to describe two future generations of the organization design model in addition to the current state. The date January 1, 1997 was chosen because that was the target date set for completing implementation of the shared services concept. The year 2001 was

FIGURE 4.1 *Multigeneration Organization Design*

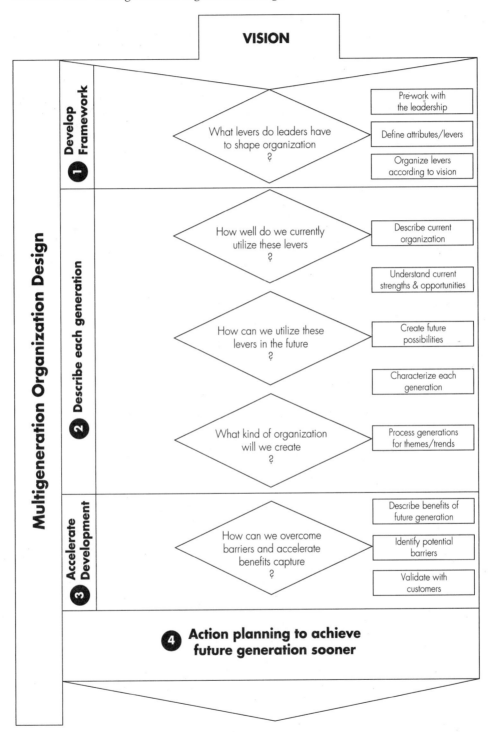

chosen because the leaders felt that it was far enough into the future to allow examination of trends in comparison to the current model and 1997 model.

Leaders needed to be educated about their role in the process and facilitators needed to be educated on how the leaders view the organization and understand the leaders' perspective on the issues and challenges that the organization faces. It is the leaders' responsibility to share with one another their aspirations for the organization, how these aspirations will be reflected in the organization design, and their commitment to implementing the design that they co-develop. The primary role of the core team was to ensure that leaders were appropriately engaged in the process and that the process would successfully enable the leaders to accomplish their objective.

Key Question: What Levers Do Leaders Have to Shape the Organization?

Twenty-four of Amoco's top leaders, including the SSMC and internal customers, were engaged to define key organizational attributes of the Shared Services organization. Individual and small group sessions were conducted to identify the key attributes or levers that the leaders have to successfully manage and develop their respective organizations. A discussion draft of over thirty potential management levers was distributed to selected leaders who whittled the list down to twelve. This list was further pruned to nine.

The pruning process was facilitated by organizing the attributes according to the Shared Services vision. Only those attributes that strongly linked to one of the three vision elements were used. Examples of these attributes include: capability to provide professional excellence (Excellence), identifying the primary focus of how a group would add value (Cost Leadership), and reinforcing alignment with customer strategies (Customer Focus). The emphasis was placed on identifying *key* levers, those deemed to have the most impact in moving the organization, not *all* levers. It was felt that this would help the leaders concentrate on the most important areas that they can leverage for organizational change.

Step Two: Describe Each Generation

The second step in the multigeneration organization design process is to describe each generation in terms of key organizational attributes. A two-day facilitated session was conducted in April 1994 with twenty-four of Amoco's top leaders, including the SSMC and customer representatives. The intended outcome of the session was to describe a vivid, compelling future state of Shared Services and commit to accelerating its development. The agenda of this session was geared to engage in dialogue guided by a nine (attributes) by three (generations) matrix. Using the vision as a touchstone, the participants extrapolated each of nine organizational attributes to describe the current state and two potential future states of Shared Services: January 1, 1997 and 2001. The current state and future generations were developed by exploring how each attribute could be leveraged to develop the organization and then having the group summarize the discussion.

Figure 4.2 presents some of the outcomes of these discussions with the attributes or levers organized by the Shared Services vision. This figure represents summaries of three of the nine attributes of what were highly detailed and extensive discussions. These discussions focused on the evolution of the vision in terms of excellence, cost leadership, and customer focus.

Key Question: How Well Do We Currently Utilize These Levers?

One of the areas under the vision heading of Excellence that the leadership group felt offers leverage to develop their organization was the "capability to provide professional excellence." It was observed that most groups were currently in the process of building functional expertise. Most of these groups were newly formed with the creation of Shared Services. Building functional expertise was considered critical to quickly establish credibility with the customers.

Cost leadership was viewed by Amoco's internal business customers as the primary means by which Shared Services suppliers may add value. The SSMC group conceded that the current emphasis on cost allocation was necessary and appropriate. The intention was for all product and service costs to be allocated to business customers. This required business processing information systems to be upgraded to provide this detailed information on a timely basis. Business customers reviewed this information and consulted with Shared Services providers to appropriately budget for the service.

Customer focus is of paramount importance for every supplier. A necessary ingredient for this is for the supplier to be aligned with customer strategies. Currently, most suppliers were in a steep learning curve with understanding customer strategies. The difficulty of this task was compounded by the fact that Amoco, as a vertically integrated oil and gas enterprise, has seventeen business groups comprised of over ninety business units. Each of these has a strategy or operating plan. Therefore, while understanding customer strategies seemed on the surface to be straightforward enough, the sheer number of strategies made this task a daunting one.

Key Question: How Can We Utilize These Levers in the Future?

With the current state of the organization described in terms of the nine attributes, attention turned to describing the future states of the organization. Each of the nine attributes was reviewed again to see how they could be leveraged to create the Shared Services organization of the future.

Returning to Figure 4.2 and the capability to provide professional excellence, the challenge in the immediate future seemed to be to focus on adding value in internal

FIGURE 4.2 *Key Organizational Attributes or Levers*

Page 3
Page 2
Page 1

Multigeneration Organization Design

VISION	ATTRIBUTE EXAMPLES	CURRENT ORGANIZATION	GENERATION 1: 1997	GENERATION 2: 2001
EXCELLENCE	Capability to provide professional excellence	Shape ourselves: Build functional expertise	Shape customers: Add value in internal customer organization through technical excellence	Shape industry: Create sustainable competitive advantage for customers
COST LEADERSHIP	Primary focus of adding value	Cost allocations: All products and service costs allocated to business customers	Demonstrate value: Benchmark externally provided services to show cost advantage of internally provided service	Share risk: Customers and suppliers share risks of partnership success
CUSTOMER FOCUS	Alignment with customer strategies	Communicate strategies: Suppliers fully understand all customer strategies	Identify themes: Examine strategies to find common themes of how to add value	Co-develop strategies: Customers and suppliers co-develop strategy for mutual success of partnership

customer organizations through technical excellence. Technology has been an acknowledged strength of Amoco. Many Shared Services leaders identified opportunities to leverage technologies to enable customers to achieve their business objectives. It was felt, however, that Shared Services could do more. Discussion soon centered on how to shape the oil and gas industry through the creation of sustainable competitive advantage for Shared Services customers.

Referring to Cost Leadership, the primary way in which Shared Services thought that they could add value in the near future was by bench marking with non-Amoco service providers. This would indicate the competitiveness of internal pricing. Lower net cost of an internally provided service as compared to an externally provided service would demonstrate real value to business customers or drive internal change. There was general consensus, however, that Amoco could not "save itself to prosperity." Being a low-cost provider is certainly important. Ultimately, however, the participants felt that a true partnership between customers and suppliers would generate the most value for the customer. In this way, cost drivers in the customer business process could be surfaced and managed. Customers and suppliers would share the risk—and rewards—of partnership success.

Increasing customer focus through alignment with customer strategies presented a challenge to supplier and customer alike. These strategies run the gamut from strong growth orientation on one end of the spectrum to asset depreciation and divestiture on the other end of the spectrum. How might customers organize these strategies to better align products and services? In the near term it was thought to be important to identify themes or trends that may run throughout these strategies. This would highlight ways that suppliers could focus on customer groupings or segments to add value.

Organizing these strategies did seem to be important but insufficient to gain full leverage from the partnership. Success of the customer-supplier partnership must be mutual. Suppliers, therefore, need to do more than merely react to customer strategies. Ultimately, customers and suppliers need to co-develop strategies to maximize the capabilities of each to reinforce the mutual success of their partnership.

Key Question: What Kind of Organization Will We Create?
This discussion continued to address how well all nine organization attributes or levers were currently utilized, how these levers could be utilized in the future, and ultimately, the kind of organization that the group wanted to create in the future. Dialogue about the current organizational state helped to better understand current strengths and improvement opportunities. Participants discovered that they shared many issues and problems and created a common ground to address these issues. Participants were encouraged to reflect upon their aspirations for their organization to stimulate ideas for the future.

Facilitators guided the discussion of each generation to also uncover themes and trends for how the Shared Services organization could develop. The following represents one of many examples of themes that emerged during discussions about what Shared Services providers should be selling to customers. Currently, it was felt that providers are selling their *time*, expressed as billing hours or days. Selling time in this way, however, has apparently distracted many customers from better understanding how the providers add value and tended to concentrate more on the cost of the provider's time. Shared Services providers wanted to move away from selling time to selling *products*. Value-added outcomes would be emphasized in contrast to just looking at delivery cost. Ideally, though, providers want to be seen as selling *process*; that is, to be valued as a true partner by their customers as contributing to their core work process and creating value for their customer's customer. Customers and suppliers could together look deeply into the customer's core work process to identify and manage those cost drivers that unnecessarily increase demand for support services.

Step Three: Accelerate Development

With the current and future states of Shared Services described, the challenge was to accelerate the development of Shared Services and realize the 2001 organization sooner.

Key Question: How Can We Overcome Barriers and Accelerate Benefits Capture?

The benefits of the 2001 model were described, as well as potential barriers to achieving the future state. Many of the benefits of the Shared Services concept came from creating a strong customer-supplier partnership. Examples of benefits included developing more services that delivered breakthrough performance and offering customers "one stop shopping" with more integrated service solutions to customer problems. Increased product development was critically important to many Shared Services providers. It was felt that the future state model would provide more opportunities for targeted investment in developing resources and new services.

The name of the game for Shared Services was identified as value creation for customers. Value creation was operationally defined as: maintaining organizational capability, reducing operating cost, and increasing value in line business operations. Shared Services adds value by maintaining functional capability across fourteen functional areas. The service is there when it is needed. Customers know how to easily access the service, and they do not have to take time away from their business to shop around to select vendors for the service.

Reduced operating cost is the perennial challenge for service providers but also an important source of value creation. A dollar saved in buying a support service can presumably be spent on a core work area, where the return on this investment will be greater. Service providers demonstrate value by realizing a lower unit cost for a service than an outside vendor would charge for a comparable service.

The participants viewed increasing value in line business operations as perhaps the greatest source where service providers could add value. It was also felt that this was the least tapped source for value creation. Selected Shared Services providers could integrate their services and provide integrated solutions to customer problems. Audit, Information Systems, and Human Resources consulting could, for example, join forces to provide comprehensive reengineering for a given line business customer. Value could be created not only because this reengineering service would be delivered at a lower cost than from what might be expected from an outside vendor, but also because there would be significant financial return on the investment that would impact the customers bottom line.

There were many formidable barriers to successful implementation of Shared Services that the group identified. Examples included how to integrate expertise cross-functionally and how to minimize bureaucracy. Participants recognized the need to share best practices across the organization and to incorporate the learnings into the fabric of their business. On the other hand, no one could afford an elaborate infrastructure to facilitate cross-functional communication. Dialogue focused on how the group could overcome these barriers and accelerate benefits capture. Using the organizational attributes or levers as a guide, the group committed itself to accelerate the development of this partnership.

While the successive generations represented a logical extension of the current organization, the group challenged itself to find ways to skip the 1997 generation model and accelerate development of Shared Services. Was it really necessary, for example, to spend years to shape customers through application of technical excellence? Perhaps Shared Services providers could partner with customers now to help shape the industry. This partnership would help create sustainable competitive advantage that would redefine the requirements for technical excellence.

The groups also questioned why more could not be done now to ensure that customers and suppliers share risks of partnership success. Potential modifications of variable incentive pay were discussed. Also, rather than spending time organizing customer strategies by themes or groupings, why not have customers and suppliers co-develop customer strategies? An important element of these strategies could be to find ways sooner to unlock synergy for joint product development. Challenging the assumptive base of the 1997 generation removed conceptual barriers to accelerating the achievement of the 2001 generation.

Step Four: Action Planning

A plan was developed that specified actions to be taken by the participants as a group as well as by each functional service organization. Functional organizations committed to incorporating the results into on-going strategy development efforts. Extensive validation of the results and conclusions with customers and constituents were also planned. Many customers had expressed concern about the cost of developing Shared Services infrastructure. Customer review was critical to ensure that any incremental investment in Shared Services would provide an appropriate return.

Accelerating the implementation of the shared services concept would require broad-based understanding and support from the organization. A detailed booklet was written that captured the ideas, models, and directions for Shared Services and hundreds of copies were distributed throughout the organization. E-mail, staff meetings, and other media avenues were utilized to communicate the results. Periodic Shared Services Management Council meetings have continued the dialogue and reinforced the acceleration of the Shared Services action plan. An important part of this plan was to continue to better define value creation and explore more how Shared Services can create value for their line business customers.

CONCLUSION

The vivid portrait of Amoco Shared Services 2001 created excitement about the future and brought into focus how the fourteen Shared Services functional organizations could pull together to create their future. The vision became clearer and compelling. Shared Services would be viewed as a true business partner by their customers—sharing risk, enjoying rewards, and reshaping the industry. Functional boundaries became viewed as permeable, allowing the passage of information and resources and unlocking synergy for product development and value creation for the customer. Commitments were made to accelerate the development of Shared Services and make this exciting future reality happen sooner.

EPILOGUE

Worldwide downward pressure on oil prices ushered in a new round of oil industry consolidation in the late 1990s. In 1998, British Petroleum bought Amoco in what was announced as a "merger of equals." The new company, BP Amoco, based in London, England, valued Amoco's marketing clout and brand image in the United States as well as its physical assets. The Shared Services organizations were not valued as strategic assets and were looked at even more aggressively for potential cost savings. As a result, some of these Shared Services organizations were greatly reduced, with the work either being eliminated or shifted to BP's support functions. In fact, by clearly separating support work from the core business, the shared service concept facilitated the dismemberment of Amoco's support organizations. And the beat goes on.

PART *III*

Change Directed at Teams

Kaizen: Accelerating Continuous Improvement

Bob Demaree and
Sander J. Smiles

INTRODUCTION

Ever since the United States felt the impact of global competition—and especially Japanese competition—America's industrial leadership has looked for ways to continuously lower costs and decrease new product development cycle time. The Total Quality Movement (TQM) ushered in a wide array of statistically based, root cause problem-solving techniques. Quality teams would relentlessly track down root causes for problems with manufacturing, product development, service quality, and other business areas. These problem-solving efforts often took months or years to complete and required extensive documentation.

Global competition has also been relentless, requiring business problems to be identified and fixed quickly. Many businesses no longer have the luxury of time for a full-blown TQM project. Consequently, business leaders are embracing Kaizen as an effective and speedy problem-solving approach. Kaizen events produce major business improvements in a fraction of time that other TQM methods would require. Kaizen is a classic example of "think small, deliver big." Bring together a few key people with a stake in the problem for a few days, employ innovative problem-solving tools, stay focused, and produce tangible business benefits. This chapter will show how Kaizen events can be implemented anywhere in business, from the open factory floor to the inner cubicles of service industries.

The term *Kaizen* has been translated in many ways over the years. A literal translation involves two Japanese words: *Kai* (to break apart, modify; to change) and *Zen* (think, make good or better). Combined, they form *Kaizen*, which means to break something into its component parts and think of ways to do it better. A fundamental assumption of Kaizen is that a business process can be improved by breaking it down into smaller parts and analyzing them for improvement. The generally accepted definition of Kaizen is limited to just continuous improvement. The actual definition is more of a spirit that whatever one is doing, one can do better. The following working definition demonstrates how this spirit is transformed into a reality:

> *Kaizen*: The aggressive and immediate upgrade of workplace methods on a real time, "Do It Now" basis. It enables everyone to continuously recognize, categorize, and eliminate waste so they can satisfy their customers.

The Kaizen event evolved from this action-oriented philosophy with the goal of solving problems quickly and eliminating *Muda*—the Japanese term for waste—or anything the customer will not pay for and anything that does not show up in the final product. In traditional TQM, this process would take place over several months or years with problems being extensively studied and measured, and incremental improvements being made.

What makes the Kaizen event format so powerful is that it allows a team the time to *focus* on a particular area for improvement, and make *real-time* changes using quality improvement tools. The improvements are based on the analysis of data collected from the targeted workplace. This results orientation, within a narrow time frame, creates a very strong structural tension within the team that gives it tremendous energy and focus to reach its goals.

Today, Kaizen events are conducted in three- to five-day increments, and business results are achieved immediately. One company slashed its Work in Process (WIP) in one production cell 89% and cycle time by 79%. Results like these are commonplace and translate into significant savings that have an immediate impact on a company's bottom line.

Nissan Motor Company was a pioneer in Kaizen and introduced a two-day Kaizen event in the late 1970s and then exported it to its U.S. plants. In the U.S. plants, the programs evolved into five-day programs. No matter the length, the principles have always been the same:

- Explain the goals.
- Explain how to collect the data.
- Identify how to begin to implement change.
- Implement the changes.
- Share with management the solutions and progress made.

This chapter will enable the reader to understand the ingredients necessary to initiate a Kaizen event and conclude with some success examples. Conducting Kaizen events requires experience with the process and the tools necessary to collect the data and implement the identified solutions. To accomplish this goal the reader will look at the preplanning and organization of a Kaizen event, key success factors, change issues, leadership roles, and post events necessary to keep the momentum of the immediate successes going.

PREPLANNING

Given the level of commitment required for Kaizen, it is necessary to carefully assess the targeted work area before a Kaizen event is held. On the technical level, this requires the collection and analysis of pertinent baseline data to determine if significant and immediate improvements can be accomplished.

On the social level, it is important to assess the area's readiness for a Kaizen event. In particular, the senior leadership must fully understand and approve the scope and nature of the Kaizen event. Their support is critical at all phases of the event. Management needs to sanction the event during the Preplanning Phase and approve the necessary resources to conduct it. They also will help to create the support and backing for the event. Often, management will have access to key information that will be helpful in planning the event. For example, they may have knowledge about the future strategic direction for an area that may preclude a Kaizen event being done, such as the machines in the designated areas that are under review and will be moved to another location.

A key action in this phase is briefing the entire work area on the goals and nature of the upcoming Kaizen event. During the briefing, the work area's members can be solicited for their ideas and thoughts on the Kaizen's area of focus. Involving the workers is an obvious but often overlooked way to minimize the resistance the group may have to any changes from the very beginning of the project. Often, the individuals in the Kaizen work area will have solid practical ideas for eliminating waste. A good question to ask in these sessions is: "If you could change one thing in your workplace, what would it be?" Very often the answer to this kind of question leads to promising areas of waste elimination and process improvements. Other points to be made during the employee briefing include:

- The results of a Kaizen are meant to improve the workplace (i.e., to make it a better place to work in, as well as to increase productivity).
- The event's objective is to make peoples' jobs more effective and safer, which in the long run will result in the company saving money.

- The Kaizen is not aimed at reducing headcount. If the company wants to achieve all of the possible returns or payoffs of a Kaizen event, assurances will be needed that people will not lose their jobs when significant efficiencies are achieved.

This Preplanning Phase is vital to the success of the Kaizen event. Setting the proper expectations for the Kaizen is a key success factor. It is accomplished by bringing together management and the leaders of the work area and communicating a clear set of expectations and goals for the event. Setting improvement goals in the 70% to 90% range are not uncommon. The goals might seem overly aggressive or seemingly outrageous, but these "stretch" goals force the Kaizen team to do "out-of-the-box" thinking and to look for the "second right answer" because the first solutions may only produce minimal improvements. Establishing clarity on the scope of the corrective actions is also important. For example, in raising productivity in a manufacturing center, the option of adding to the headcount or making large capital improvements were not viable. The operations manager clearly stated these conditions at the outset so that employees would not first turn to the "easy" solutions of adding people or throwing money at the problem.

Team Selection

Once the scope and goals of the Kaizen are set and approved by management, the selection of the team is the next critical step. The Kaizen team should be composed of six to eight people who come from the targeted work areas and also from outside of them. The individuals from the work areas bring a deep knowledge of how the work areas operate on a day-to-day basis. This experience is very important and provides the necessary information to make sound decisions based on what actually happens in the work areas. Equally important are the team members who do not have any firsthand knowledge of the targeted areas. They bring "fresh eyes" to the event. They are able to ask very basic questions as to how the work areas function. More important they require the process experts to provide a thorough explanation of how the work is conducted. They will ask simple, yet powerful questions such as "Why do you do it that way?" or "How does this process work?" These questions are effective because they often reveal the unquestioned assumptions of how the work is being accomplished. Often the targeted area(s) is working with assumptions that have not been questioned for years. The process experts often reply to the "fresh eyes" questions with "we've always done it that way" or "I'm not sure why we do it that way." These kinds of questions force the experts to explain the process so that everyone can understand it.

A key factor in selecting fresh-eyes team members is participants' willingness to get involved with the Kaizen activities needed to make the event a success. People from finance, sales, engineering, or human resources can gain great exposure to what happens on the shop floor and to the people who work there. Including fresh-eyes participants who are expert in the problem area being addressed is helpful. However, the experts must understand the collaborative nature of the Kaizen event. Joining with the attitude that they are going to tell everyone how to do their jobs better will be counterproductive and not successful. Besides team members, a Kaizen team will need to have a process owner and a facilitator. Both of these roles will be explained later during the team-building section.

One final area needs to be addressed in the Preplanning Phase. The team must arrange for the key company support areas such as maintenance, information services, engineering, and facilities to be available during the event. Having these areas ready to aid the Kaizen team quickly is vital to maintaining the team's momentum during the Kaizen event.

THE KAIZEN EVENT

With the Preplanning Phase completed, the next phase is the actual Kaizen event. The Kaizen team goes through three distinct stages in this phase: Training, Data Collection and Analysis, and Implementation.

Training

A Kaizen training session gives the team an introduction to the skills and concepts necessary for a successful event: Kaizen tools and techniques, Kaizen philosophy, flow manufacturing, and team development. The objective of the training is to enable the team members to achieve success and be able to apply the tools during the event.

The learning begins with defining Kaizen and why this process is being used. It is put into context for the learner as a business strategy that seeks to help meet the ever-increasing requirement of the marketplace. Customers are demanding that companies reduce costs, shorten delivery times, and improve quality. A Kaizen event gives a team dedicated time to focus on meaningful improvements through applied common sense. It closes the time gap between learning, action, and improvement and most importantly demonstrates that concrete change is achievable in the workplace.

From the very beginning, the lesson learned during a Kaizen event involves the actual changing of the workplace to improve it. Today's work force has gone through a great many improvement and change programs that often did not effect meaningful change in the workplace. As a result, team members and affected work area individuals approach a Kaizen event somewhat skeptical about actual change taking place.

Kaizen Training Topics

Every Kaizen event has ten rules or operating principles that convey the overall spirit of the event (see Table 5.1). Each principle is reviewed with the team. This effort is especially important for the team members who have not experienced a Kaizen event

TABLE 5.1   *Ten Rules of Kaizen*

1. Discard conventional ideas.
2. Think of how to do it, not why it cannot be done.
3. Do not make excuses; challenge current practices.
4. Do not wait for perfection; improve the area right away.
5. Correct mistakes at once; do not harm the customer.
6. Optimize current equipment and resources; creativity before capital.
7. Wisdom is brought about when faced with hardship and when all can see and feel the waste.
8. Ask "why" five times and seek root causes.
9. Seek the wisdom of ten rather than the knowledge of one.
10. Kaizen never stops.

previously and who may initially view it solely as a few days of problem solving. Thinking of a Kaizen event as just an extended problem-solving session is understandable since many of the tools and techniques are similar. However, in the Kaizen context these tools take on an immediate bias for action and results, not just providing answers.

Team Building

With the Kaizen principles in mind, the next most important aspect of the Kaizen event needs to be addressed: team building skills. For a successful Kaizen event, the participants must understand that successful teams do not happen by luck or accident. All work teams have to learn how to work together and be aware of the essential building blocks of any successful team: goals and objectives, roles and responsibilities, work processes and relationships—and the interpersonal interactions between the team members and people outside of the team. Often, a simple team-building exercise is conducted that allows the group to identify and discuss the success factors needed in a high performing team. These building blocks are then addressed one by one.

The goal of the Kaizen event is presented and explained. In other words, the target that the process owner and/or management have set is announced. Since many of the team members have been involved in the preplanning, most of the team will not be surprised. Reactions to the goal are briefly discussed with the understanding that more discussion will be held in the afternoon.

Next, roles and responsibilities during the Kaizen event are outlined. The three main roles in a Kaizen event include: facilitator, process owner, and team member. The facilitator's main role is to provide training and support on the Kaizen tools and techniques and guide the team through the Kaizen event process. Guiding the team means keeping the team focused on its goals, the data at hand, and the implementation of corrective actions that will improve the workplace during the event. Often, the facilitator will need to push the group for concrete results when they are spending too much time in the data analysis phase.

The process owner comes from the targeted work area. He or she has an in-depth knowledge of the work area and will take responsibility to lead the post-Kaizen implementation efforts. If the process owner has had previous Kaizen experience, then he or she can also take a leadership role within the Kaizen team. Team leadership often rotates throughout the team as different needs and tasks arise.

Waste and the Causes of Waste in Manufacturing

After the rules of Kaizen and key aspects of team building are covered, the Kaizen event focuses on waste. Waste in manufacturing is placed in seven categories in a Kaizen event:

1. Defective products
2. Overproduction
3. Inventories
4. Motion
5. Processing
6. Transportation
7. Waiting

Examples of each category and their causes are presented and discussed. Seeing concrete examples of waste is critical. Since the examples shown are so common, they are often not seen as waste but rather as something that has always existed in the workplace and has gained acceptance. The best way to learn that this waste is not acceptable is to conduct a manufacturing simulation in which the team is actually involved in a manufacturing process that exhibits many of these waste categories. The direct experience provides an excellent opportunity for everyone to learn how to use the various Kaizen data collection tools, such as videotaping and time observations, to quantify the data. Typically, the manufacturing simulation will follow the briefing on waste.

During the simulation and throughout the Kaizen event the facilitator emphasizes the Kaizen event's main goal: To eliminate and/or minimize waste in any way possible in order to reach the specific performance goals. It is also important to make a distinction between evaluating the process and evaluating the people in the process. The main focus of any Kaizen event is not to evaluate the people in the process but to analyze and improve the process itself. Often, this key point will have to be addressed repeatedly because most workers in the United States are not trained to look at process. Sometimes, teams will focus on the performance of the people in the process without considering the process in which they work or the baseline data collected on the process.

KAIZEN OVERVIEW

After the simulation, an overview or road map of how the entire Kaizen event process will work over the next three days is presented. Most Kaizen events of varying lengths will follow this outline:

- Identify and focus on area to improve.
- Collect baseline data.
- Document the current workflow steps.
- Identify value added effort and waste.
- Brainstorm ways to eliminate waste, simplify the process, and improve the work area.
- Implement where possible.
- Remeasure and evaluate results.
- Document best practices.

From this review the team is ready to proceed into the next critical phase, data collecting, and analysis.

DATA COLLECTION AND ANALYSIS

Following the training in the morning of the first day comes the data collection and analysis phase. To be successful, this phase should be done quickly and thoroughly. Often, the group will immediately jump into a solution mode before collecting relevant data and analyzing it. Team members who work in the targeted areas usually jump in with solutions because their experience in the work area over time has primed them to develop ideas for improvement. However, they often have never had the chance to implement them. To succeed, the group will need to stay focused on the data obtained before proposing any solutions. The old phrase "ready—aim—fire" has to be kept in mind.

Also, those Kaizen event team members not familiar with the project need to get a solid understanding of the work area and the baseline data. Their value as "fresh eyes" to the work area becomes apparent at this point. As they gain an understanding of the project work area, they can ask very basic questions that often enlighten the whole team. Their simple questions about the process often reveal great opportunities for waste elimination that would have been overlooked by those who work in the area under review. A question like "Why do you do it that way?" forces the whole Kaizen team to look deeply into a process that might have otherwise been overlooked by the "expert" on the team.

IMPLEMENTATION AND EVALUATION

By the end of the morning of the second day, the data analysis should be completed and corrective actions should be considered and ready for implementation. The three-day event itself limits the scope of the corrective actions as long as the team is planning to complete their implementations during the event. At times, the facilitator must reinforce the concept that implementation is to take place during the event. Also, the facilitator will often need to refocus the group away from corrective actions that require capital investments. The themes *do what can be done now to improve the workplace* and *limited time exists to make these improvements* will need to be reinforced. The solutions may not be perfect, but they will improve performance.

Once the corrective actions have been selected, then they need to be implemented and evaluated. They also need to be tested in the work area under normal conditions. A key step here is to do the same data collection activities that were done originally to verify solution effectiveness. This testing and evaluation documentation is also used in the management presentation.

This phase of the Kaizen event is a very powerful one for the team members, especially for those who normally work in the area. It is at this point that they truly understand that they are really going to change the workplace for the better by the actions taken, such as moving equipment, cleaning the work area, or changing work processes. The changes are physically evident and allow the team members and other work-area employees to see that positive change is possible.

DOCUMENTATION AND PRESENTATION OF SOLUTIONS

By the end of the third morning, the Kaizen team has finished collecting data on its corrective actions and has begun documenting all the improvements made, as well as any follow-up items. The documentation is very important for the training of the other operators who were part of the Kaizen team.

With the documentation completed, the presentation to management can be drafted. The facilitator normally coordinates this activity for the team and coaches the team members on the presentation they will be giving to management. This presentation on the last day is a regular and critical part of the Kaizen event. At this time, management visibly shows its support and concretely sees that Kaizen events do produce tangible results.

Reluctance amongst the team to be involved with the presentation is normal and understandable. Most of the team does not have experience making presentations of any kind, but the facilitator's coaching and a few rehearsals usually overcome any concerns. The key to reducing the anxiety is to involve the entire team in the presentation and explain that participants do not have to memorize anything. The presentations are designed to be short and to the point. Its focus is the Kaizen event goals, tools used, and the results achieved. A typical presentation takes fifteen to twenty minutes at the most. After the presentation the Kaizen team usually receives some sort of recognition from management for their participation and the results achieved.

POST-KAIZEN PHASE

Besides documenting the solutions and developing the presentation on the third day, the team needs to put together a plan on how all the improvements will be maintained or implemented. This plan must define what and when follow-up items need to be done and who will do them. Status check meetings also need to be scheduled to keep tabs on the post-Kaizen work. Because of the intensity and time commitment of the Kaizen event, there tends to be a drop-off in energy and focus after the event. It is important that the process owner with the support of management takes ownership of these items so that they do not become lost. It is good practice to establish periodic status checkpoints at which the process owner and representatives from the Kaizen team meet to review their progress with management. This progress may be reported back to the Kaizen event team and work-area participants so that they are also kept up to date. If regular work team meetings can also be established, the time can be used to communicate and update this information.

Post-Kaizen follow-up items need to be carefully considered. Often, the team generates a large number of follow-up items, fifty or more in the heat of the Kaizen event. This can leave a tremendous burden on the people who have to provide the follow-up. A key tip to a successful event is to seriously consider items in terms of the feasibility of being implemented. Some Kaizen practitioners put a thirty-day implementation limit on the follow-up items to minimize the amount of post-Kaizen work to be done. The Kaizen event is designed to allow the implementation of corrective actions during the event itself. Its purpose is not to generate long lists of action items for the future, but to eliminate waste in the workplace during the event.

MANAGING THE CHANGE ISSUES

Much of the success of implementing Kaizen rests on how engaged everyone in the work area was during the actual Kaizen event. If an effort to engage all work-area employees in the decisions about the improvements took place during the event, then less resistance to implement the improvement will be encountered. Another success factor is obtaining the work area's feedback on the improvement prior to their actual implementation. However, if this has not occurred, then there is a good chance of strong resistance from the work-area constituents. An alternative way to bring everyone into the process is to invite the entire work area to the management presentation. The other key ingredient to minimizing resistance is the role that the work-area Kaizen team members take in communicating and explaining the changes during and after the event. Often, they will need to be involved with the training of their coworkers on the new procedures developed in the Kaizen event.

KAIZEN SUCCESS STORIES

No process is perfect, but Kaizen efforts have accomplished significant results in saving time and/or money. Following are three examples that typify the process and business value of Kaizen Events.

1. *Receiving and Material Testing.* The combined efforts of a receiving area and material testing lab of a manufacturing facility produced an average cycle time of sixty-one hours to release raw material to production (from receiving dock to production floor). The Kaizen team, composed of people from both the receiving area and material testing lab plus two sets of "fresh eyes," reduced the average cycle time to twelve hours! This 80% reduction in cycle time was achieved without any capital improvements or increase in people.

2. *Machine Center Change Over.* A critical aspect of every manufacturing facility is its flexibility when switching machinery from one product configuration to another. The faster the "setup" time, the more the machine can be kept producing product. One Kaizen looked at reducing the average setup time for one machine that was forty-eight minutes. The Kaizen team was able to reduce that time to fourteen minutes after eliminating the nonvalue-adding activities. This was a 71% reduction in setup time that cost approximately $200 to implement. The productivity that resulted yielded tens of thousands of dollars a year.

3. *Laboratory Processing.* One Kaizen team was formed to look at reducing the processing time in a lab. The team reduced the lab processing time by 50% and saved $15,000 in labor costs in one year. With this saving in labor, the lab was able to increase its work in other critical areas without having to hire additional personnel.

SUMMARY

Kaizen events work and can help any area of business where a work process or a series of steps adds value to a product or service. This methodology is teachable to all types of individuals in any type of industry. The key requirement is a desire to improve a product or service and not being afraid to implement solutions quickly. Kaizen events are synonymous with taking immediate action. Analyses and studies are important, but results come from taking actions on the root causes of problems. One of the best ways to determine root cause is to ask the people who are closest to the problem or issue being reviewed. Kaizen is both a method and a spirit. One without the other will not work for very long.

SUGGESTED READINGS

Imai, M. (1997). *Gemba Kaizen: A commonsense, low-cost approach to management.* New York: McGraw-Hill.

Imai, M. (1986). *Kaizen: The key to Japan's competitive success.* New York: Random House.

Tichy, N. M., & Sherman, S. (1994). *Control your destiny or someone else will.* New York: Doubleday.

The Paradox: Doing Deep Work to Foster Spirit in Impermanent, Transient, Cross-Functional Teams

Barry Heermann

THE SEEN AND THE UNSEEN: AN INTRODUCTION

The twentieth century has brought remarkable advances in technology, transportation, and communication, but with these advances something has also been overlooked, especially in work and organizational life. Modern organizations tend to be preoccupied with form and structure, on what is "seen," with less awareness or capacity to foster the missing, the unseen. Too often we hear: "If you can't see it, it's not real" and "What can't be measured, can't be."

This thinking masquerades as being scientific, but emerging science teaches a different lesson. Physicists tell us that all of nature is made up of unseen molecular structures expressed in various rhythmic patterns. These structures are "self-organizing." From the tiniest cell to the largest system there is a "disequilibrium" that is inherently nurturing, moving toward higher and higher levels of organization.

Spiritual traditions around the world teach of a similarly unseen force residing deep within, which expresses itself in the work of humankind. Despite the understanding in scientific and spiritual domains of the unseen organization force, modern organizations address form and structure at the Newtonian level of parts, pieces, and splinters of things. We manipulate, we rearrange, we create new combinations—all at a surface level.

These manipulations are ultimately deadening, because they do not speak to that which animates work—the spirit that gives life to the organization. It is not surprising that organizations and organizational workers experience a loss of animation and diminished meaning and purpose, or that effectiveness declines when these matters are overlooked—for they are not easily quantifiable or expressed in a formula or model.

What is missing is consideration of something deeper, more essential: the ubiquitous, all inclusive unseen, or spirit, that gives life to the organization.

Consider the wisdom of the poet Lao Tzu in the ancient *Tao Te Ching* translated by Stephen Mitchell (1988):

We join spokes together in a wheel,
but it is the center hole
that makes the wagon move.
We shape clay into a pot,
but it is the emptiness inside
that holds whatever we want.
We hammer wood for a house,
but it is the inner space that
makes it livable.

A growing body of practice and research on high performance teams underscores the critical missing dimension. Peter Vaill (1989) notes:

All the case studies and other research results that have come out about excellence and peak performance confirm that both members and observers of excellent organizations consistently feel the spirit of the organization and the activity, and that this feeling of spirit is an essential part of the meaning and value that members and observers place on the activity.

The defining characteristic of the high performing team—the trait that makes a team more than the sum of its members—is "spirit." Recognizing and fostering the spirit dimension of team is emerging as a viable way to achieve organizational effectiveness. But what is this elusive quality so important to team and organization? Spirit is not separate from worldly affairs, nor is spirit some ephemeral, elusive, or ambiguous state. It is at the core of our humanity, should we choose to notice and cultivate it. Spirit contains its own source of meaning and purpose. It inspires us, catapulting us beyond self. In going beyond self, teams become inspirited. Selflessness is powerful and deeply spiritual. Out of selflessness we give ourselves freely to important work, to the service of others, or to colleagues with whom we join in work.

In moving beyond narrow self-interest, beyond the individualism that permeates our culture, the possibility of extraordinary teamwork emerges. Spirit is at the depth of this possibility, and a spirited team is the desired end state. Spirit is multifaceted, and while at some level spirit defies cognitive understanding, we can name the qualities of spirit operating within teams, and we can employ simple processes to bring spiritedness to our work. Identifying these qualities provides a common vocabulary for teams to reflect on their work together. In consultation projects with organizations such as AT&T, NCR, and LEXIS-NEXIS that inform this chapter, six qualities have been identified, worked with, and framed as "phases" of a spiral (Herrmann, 1996) (see Figure 6.1):

1. **Service—The Core Integrating Phase**
   Quality of spirit: The experience of contribution and service to others.

2. **Letting Go**
   Quality of spirit: A sense of freedom and completion that arises from being forthright and sharing with full integrity.

FIGURE 6.1 *The Team Spirit Spiral*

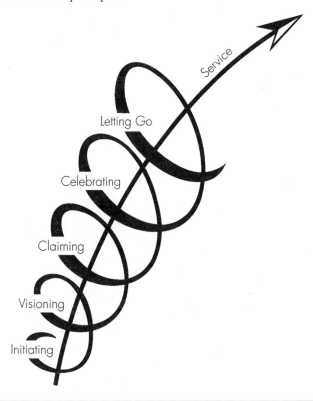

3. **Celebrating**

Quality of spirit: The presence of awe, wonder, and appreciation for the contribution of the team and team members.

4. **Claiming**

Quality of spirit: The experience of team solidarity, single-minded purpose, and clarification about what needs to be accomplished.

5. **Visioning**

Quality of spirit: An extraordinary sense of possibility for what can be created that is alive and present for the team.

6. **Initiating**

Quality of spirit: A profound sense of relationship, wherein team members feel belonging and trust in their work together.

All teams, whether consciously or unconsciously, move through and operate in all phases, linked by the critical sixth integrating component of Service. Each phase has its own unique contribution to make in realizing a spirited team. These phases operate simultaneously and interdependently. Experience in consulting shows that ordinary work groups can become spirited, high performing teams by consciously attending to each of these phases. Embracing the spirit in team, in all of its various manifestations—both its light and shadow sides—is critical to significant team and organization renewal.

The work of providing practical experiences and interventions in Fortune 500 companies, major not-for-profits, and small- and medium-sized enterprises that promote team spirit has been instructive. A firsthand knowledge of the potential for delivering a deeper level of team development, transcending individual differences, and leading to brilliant service to customers has been gained.

THE CHALLENGE: USING TEAM SPIRIT WITH HIGHLY TRANSIENT, CROSS-FUNCTIONAL TASK FORCES

Team spirit is designed for use with "intact teams," that is, existing teams and work groups within an organization. Team spirit is tailored to the type and needs of the team as it relates to their phase in the Team Spirit Spiral. For example, a team experiencing withheld communications might be supported to engage in Letting Go work to disclose and speak more openly about its disappointments and/or difficulties existing within the team. Team spirit is highly experiential so that team members have direct experience with the phase or phases of the spiral that are critical to their development.

The formulation of team spirit varies with the configuration of the team. We distinguish between conventional teams that are either startup or mature teams and cross-functional task forces: teams that are organized for short-term functions, frequently composed of persons who represent different functions and levels of the organization. In organizations that employ this form of team, employees may serve on several cross-functional teams, for varying durations and for varying lengths of time. They accomplish particular short-term outcomes and, having fulfilled those outcomes, disband. They are transient and short-lived. Frequently they are autonomous or self-directed in configuration. A complicated array of functional, temperamental, and cultural factors is often characteristic of this kind of team.

Working with teams at a deep level so that they effectively connect with, and draw from, their spirit is seemingly exacerbated by these more fluid and transitory forms of cross-functional task forces. For example, cross-functional task forces do not have the luxury of participating in periodic two-day workshops over a year or more, as is typical of conventional teams that OD consultants work with. Consider these variations of teams:

1. *Conventional startup teams* typically participate in experiences focused on the Initiating, Visioning, and Claiming phases of the Team Spirit Spiral during the first six to nine months, followed by work on the Celebrating, Letting Go, and Service phases later in their development.
2. *Conventional mature teams* have needs that are a function of their history and developmental phase in the Team Spirit Spiral. Interviews with representative team members are conducted in order to tailor interventions and experiences. Whether a startup or a mature team, a year long commitment is recommended, consisting of a series of two-day workshops offered every three to four months in order to achieve a significant shift in the spirit and performance of the team.
3. *Cross-functional task forces* place a premium on the Claiming phase of the Team Spirit Spiral because of the time-bound, project orientation of their work—that is, on role definition, task completion, and goal attainment. The absence of effective Initiating hampers the team's capacity to create powerful relationships. Similarly, without penetrating Visioning the potential of the team is significantly impeded, and giving short shrift to Celebrating and Letting Go results in disimpassioned service that results in only mediocre performance. Team spirit must be delivered consistently with the fast-paced needs of these teams, supporting team members to quickly and powerfully develop a relationship, vision, and claim to their work.

Unlike work with conventional teams, which begins by assessing team needs, identifying the phase of the Spiral that is key to the team's spirit and performance, drawing from interventions and experiences that best respond to team needs, with cross-functional task forces momentum is created by doing focused, short-term work. Here are several scenarios for how work with cross-functional teams can proceed:

- In organizations where there is a commitment to a company-wide application of team spirit, all employees are asked to complete two half-day sessions, with employees randomly assigned to introductory team spirit sessions. During the two sessions, employees come to understand the dimension of spirit in team, and they participate in a series of experiential activities where they come into contact with the qualities of spirit expressed in the Team Spirit Spiral. Following this common experience with Team Spirit, they participate in follow-up half-day sessions, as necessary, working with that aspect of the Spiral where the most attention is needed.

- In many organizations there is a commitment to team development, but it is provided on an optional basis versus a mandatory program. Given the pattern of highly transient cross-functional teams as described previously, this context poses an even greater challenge. These teams have such a predominant focus on Claiming (i.e., goals and roles, project completion, and the like), it is difficult for teams to address their own need to engage in cohesive team development. For these teams, organizations can provide a half-day team spirit session that acquaints them with the Team Spirit Spiral, engaging them in a simple diagnostic process. The diagnostic process has team members seeing concretely where their spirit is full and buoyant and where it is depleted and diminished.

In either of these scenarios, teams develop an awareness that sensitizes them to the unseen dimensions of which they were formerly unaware and which they lacked a vocabulary for discerning and understanding. More importantly, out of this experience they "own" the value of the journey to enhance team spirit. These teams have the opportunity to participate at a later time in concise, highly focused interventions and experiences (typically two to three hours in duration) tailored to support them in embracing a particular quality of spirit in the Team Spirit Spiral that is the key to their performance and success. Cross-functional task forces working on projects over more extensive periods of time may elect to participate in two-day workshop experiences used commonly with conventional teams.

SUMMARY

Despite remarkable technological advances in this age, something has also been overlooked, especially in organization life: the deep, inner knowledge of the spirit. Spirit has powerful implications for extraordinary team and organization performance. The

Team Spirit Spiral identifies qualities of spirit that contribute to team performance. Simple processes are made available to foster spirited, high-performing teams. However, the challenge to foster spirited teams posed by short duration, cross-functional task forces is formidable. Accordingly, a team development process has been created which is tailored to the fast-paced needs of these teams, permitting them to quickly and powerfully initiate, vision, claim, celebrate, and let go—to achieve the highest possible standards of service.

SUGGESTED READINGS

Heermann, B. (1997). *Building team spirit: Activities for inspiring and energizing teams.* New York: McGraw-Hill.

Heermann, B. (1996). Spirit in team. In J. Renesch & B. DeFoore (Eds.), *The new bottom line: bringing heart and soul to business.* San Francisco: New Leaders Press/Sterling and Stone.

Lao Tzu. (1988). *Tao te ching.* Stephen Mitchell, tr. New York: Harper & Row.

Vaill, P. (1989). *Managing as a performing art.* San Francisco: Jossey-Bass.

P A R T   *IV*

Change Directed
at Individuals

Fast Cycle Learning

Darryl Strickler
and Bryan Law

*No amount of sophistication is going to allay the fact that all your knowledge is
about the past and all your decisions are about the future.*

—Ian E. Wilson

This chapter presents a perspective on developing and implementing experiential learning environments that have a faster cycle time and are much more effective than the training and education programs traditionally offered within organizations. Traditional education is characterized by the classic lecture and associated activity approach to education. *Experiential* learning completely breaks the mold of traditional education by enabling learners to control their own learning in an environment that simulates their work "reality." The intention of this chapter is to challenge some fundamental beliefs about how best to develop and implement learning in organizational settings. The concepts and examples contained in this chapter represent successful OD work in organizations that face real-world problems and issues and represent proven methodology that has worked in a variety of organizational settings.

BREAKING THE MOLD

There is a new paradigm for learning. It is the ability to rapidly acquire, assimilate, and apply new knowledge within the workplace—the ability to *learn how to learn*. This is a significant change from the old paradigm of success replication. The old learning paradigm depends upon documenting processes, dividing them into instructional modules, and having participants repeat the desired performance—basically having learners replicate what has worked in the past. This approach is sequential in nature and takes an extended period of time to complete. People today must *learn at the speed of change*. The traditional instructional systems designer would say: "No problem, we'll just staff up the training department to create enough courses and workshops to stay ahead of the rapid half-life of knowledge." This approach may work in limited technical training, such as installing an Oracle database or processing an insurance claim. However, these instances are becoming fewer and farther in between. The quickening pace of global business requirements and customer expectations now requires the Oracle database installer to also become a technical consultant, or the claims processor to also become a sales representative charged with bringing in additional revenue. These are examples of performance goals where there is no *one* way to be successful. Multiple variables must be mastered.

Mastering multiple variables in today's fast-paced business climate requires people to acquire skills that combine the art and science of performing their work. These skills must be developed in a new way that emphasizes the target performance—but still allows for individual creativity. Additionally, individuals today not only need to learn greater quantities of complex art and science knowledge and skills to be successful, they need to learn how to learn independent of the training department. The success replication approach is inadequate and inappropriate for most of today's "knowledge workers" who must make critical decisions and invent new solutions to new problems that arise every day. Such workers need learning opportunities in which they can gain new insights and learn how to learn in order to keep abreast of rapidly changing circumstances in which they must operate.

UNCOVERING YOUR ASSUMPTIONS

It is very tempting to simply proceed with a "this is what we have found to be successful, so you try it yourself" type of approach. But this approach is the old success replication model, and it would not serve current organizational needs very well. Instead, the focus will be on developing a fresh approach to solving the learning needs within an organization, an approach that is the learners' own and will work for their specific situation. The following goal *may* suit the readers' needs. (If not, learners should set their own goal before going any further.)

> The examples, concepts, and illustrations in this chapter, along with the reader's own experience will enable the reader to think actively and creatively in constructing a new approach to creating learning initiatives. Embracing a new approach will require the reader to uncover and challenge assumptions he or she may have about

how people learn. Creating a new learning environment is accomplished by following five components of an experience-based learning event: establishing needs, creating the goal, designing the learning event or environment, enacting reality, and assessing the results.

1. Establishing Needs

The contrast between an experience-based learning approach and the traditional approach to establishing learning needs is significant. Consider for a moment how learning goals are typically determined. People usually known as "instructional designers" spend an inordinate amount of time and resources gathering and carefully documenting data from observations, interviews, and focus groups in a process usually referred to as a "needs assessment." So far so good, except that the people who do this data collection frequently operate from a "deficiency model" that negatively biases what they are looking for. This approach focuses on what needs to be fixed, and therefore—knowingly or unknowingly—influences the outcomes. An "unappreciative inquiry" leads to under-appreciating peoples learning accomplishments and skill building needs. Secondly, and equally distressing, is that the mountain of data collected is then rolled up, aggregated, and summarized in such a way that it no longer represents what any one person actually does or needs to learn how to do.

In many instances, a better alternative for assessing learning needs may be a culturally sensitive ethnographic study, similar to what anthropologists do when they study a group of native people living in natural environments. Such studies conducted in workplace environments result in a much more accurate and unbiased representation of the culture and what people actually do in the workplace. Thus, this approach provides a clearer picture of what must be done to affect significant changes within that culture to achieve specific organizational goals. When contrasted with the type of force-fitting and shoe-horning that usually takes place under the banner of needs assessment, the data from ethnographic studies provides information that is far richer and much more useful as a starting point for inquiry and learning.

2. Creating the Goal

Because most learning is incidental, spontaneous, largely unplanned, and takes place within a context of meaning supplied by the learner, it does not come with a stated goal or visible label attached to it. We learn for very personal reasons, sometimes whether or not we consciously want to. We learn because we need to grow and change, and because it is natural to do so. One person's reasons for learning may be very different from another's, and although two individuals may appear to be learning the same thing, they may attach very different meanings to what they learn. This being the case, it would be ideal if everyone created his or her own personalized goals for learning. (The evidence is that people *do* create their own *internal* goals or reasons in any case, even if not consciously.)

All *organized* learning initiatives, on the other hand, obviously need to have a stated goal, otherwise how would anyone know what they were supposed to accomplish and, more importantly, whether they really *wanted* to accomplish it. For example, let us say that you as a learning professional were asked to create an experience-based learning event that simulated the actual sales process in which sales people (the learners in this case) sell services to a client. Your learning event would feature a series of meetings with executives from a simulated client company and other simulated activities. The overall goal of the learning event would be to create an offer-and-value proposition that is based on a clear understanding of the customer's business needs. This learning goal has several important characteristics. First, it is directly related to what these particular sales people do every working day. It is not a contrived learning goal or enabling objective that some clever person just concocted—it is what these sales people must do to make their sales quotas and thereby keep their jobs! For this reason, it is very relevant to them.

The second important characteristic of this learning goal is that it is holistic, not atomistic. It incorporates and subsumes a myriad of specific skills, knowledge, and attitudes, and it focuses on what must be accomplished over a finite period of time. It is not a partial picture of what they must do, but the whole picture, wrapped in a meaningful, work-related context. Finally, in what may seem to be a contradiction in terms, this goal does not so much describe an "end state," but a journey. Any goal worth attaining should come with a built-in "receding horizon," that is, be upwardly adjustable, but still appropriate, as learners increase their level of competence. It must always be just out of reach; otherwise what is there to strive for?

3. Designing the Learning Event or Environment
Simulating Reality of the Workplace

Central to an experience-based learning event is replicating the "reality" of the workplace. Reality is, of course, relative to each individual. Reality is a composite picture that incorporates numerous variables, some of which, such as using a new process, approach, or software program, can be controlled, changed, or manipulated during a planned learning event. Other variables such as client characteristics, work dynamics, and internal company processes may remain unchanged. To simulate reality within a learning environment, all of these variables—controlled and uncontrolled—must be recreated or represented in some way in order to immerse the learner in the reality of their work. Ethnographic data is essential for this to happen. Peoples' perception of the value of any learning event in which they are asked to participate is often directly related to how closely that event approximates their own specific version of reality and the extent to which they believe they can apply what they learn "next Monday morning." Capturing and modeling reality within the learning event is undoubtedly the most significant component for the successful transfer of what was learned to the actual work setting. The more closely reality is represented or simulated in the learning environment, the easier it is for people to apply what they learn on the job.

It is equally important to recognize that most people do their work every day without the formal presence of an instructor. It is, therefore, necessary to simulate the same situation during learning events to create an environment in which the learners have control over their own learning, either individually or as a member of a team, just as they do while they are working. Allowing learners to control their own pace and decide on which areas to focus and investigate enables them to develop learning-to-learn skills. This is done through assessing, planning, and monitoring their own learning strategies. In addition, learner-controlled learning allows individuals to challenge their own mental models for processing new information and understanding their world.

Example: Application of Learning

The following example illustrates how learning can be supported while allowing for individual needs to be achieved. Using the simulated sales motion that was briefly described above, the overall goal is to create an offer and value proposition that is based on a clear understanding of the customer's business needs. To accomplish this goal, the learners (in this case, the members of a sales account team) use a grid to analyze and plan the sales strategy within their accounts. Figure 7.1 presents this grid.

FIGURE 7.1 *Sales Strategy Planning Tool*

	What do we know?	What do we need to know?	What's next?
Players			
Needs			
Link Between Need and Solution			
Differentiation			
Value			

After each sales call meeting with a client executive, members of the account team use the grid to fill in the information that they have gathered, discuss the unfolding sales situation, and then decide what they need to do or find out next. The ultimate reason for using a performance support tool like the sales grid in Figure 7.1 is for the sales people (i.e., the learners) to apply what they are learning directly to their own work setting. To do that, they must be given opportunities to practice the new learning in exactly the same way that it will be used on the job. This grid then becomes not just a tool for the learning session but a tool for learning that gained value in the session and will be utilized henceforth in the real work setting.

Creating Dissonance

The most intensive type of genuinely self-motivated learning takes place as a result from either making mistakes or just feeling uncomfortable with what we know. However, most professionals are moderately comfortable with what they know, and although they probably have the sense that there is certainly more they could learn, they are generally satisfied with what they already know. So how can those who are responsible for learning get people within organizations to want to learn new concepts or behaviors, or otherwise change in positive ways? The answer is straightforward but not necessarily simple: Create just enough cognitive dissonance within the work environment or within learning events so that learners feel that they are *not* satisfied with what they already know. This feeling of discomfort must last long enough until learners can supply their own internal motivation to learn new behaviors or approaches to a situation.

Returning to the example of the simulated sales motion to illustrate this point, there are few groups of people who appear more confident with what they know (and can do) than sales people. If within the learning environment of the simulated sales motion they are asked to make sales calls on client executives (something they do every day), they are not too likely to believe that they need to learn anything new or behave any differently than they usually do in such situations. But if they encounter a client executive within the simulated sales motion who is very different from the executives they usually call on—a client who wants to test the salesperson's business and technical knowledge—then even the most supremely confident sales professional will move quickly out of his or her level of comfort. Once this happens, and probably not *unless* this happens, the salesperson becomes truly internally motivated to learn new skills, acquire new industry knowledge, or discover a completely new approach to the sales motion. Once generated, this type of motivation does not end with the completion of the training event, but carries over directly to the workplace.

4. Enacting Reality

Building Skills, Knowledge, and Insight

After helping people create the motivation to learn (the *why*), the next question arises: What skills, knowledge, and insights should people develop as a result of participating in the learning events? It is vital to design learning events in such a way that they make it possible for people to attain new knowledge, develop new skills, and apply the skills and knowledge within the context of how the skills and knowledge will be used. This then makes it possible (and more likely) that people will develop new insights that grow out of experience. The interrelationship between knowledge, skills, and insight is represented in Figure 7.2.

Knowledge capital that people may need to be successful in their work can be distributed and managed in the form of print material, videos, CD-ROMs, and Inter- and Intranet Web pages. There is little need, and even less justification, to present information to people through live lecture. Examples of knowledge capital that might be provided to participants during a learning event include content specific documentation, supporting documentation, and prerecorded subject matter expertise.

Skills will be developed, refined, and practiced as a result of the learners' total immersion in the activities that take place during the learning event, from feedback on individual performance from coaches or mentors, and from self-assessment.

Insight will be attained as a result of participants monitoring and reflecting upon their own overall performance. This is enabled through facilitated reflection sessions in which participants take a time-out from the simulation or other learning

FIGURE 7.2 *Interrelationship Among Knowledge, Skills, and Insight*

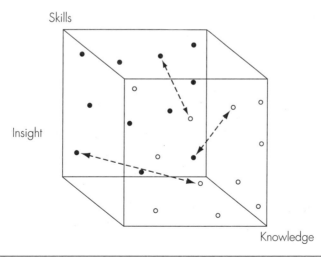

event and assess for themselves what has worked well, what they would do differently next time, and how they might handle similar situations they encounter in their work setting.

Coordinating the Experience-based Learning Event: The Learning Coach

Coordinating an experience-based learning event from the role of a learning coach is somewhat like being the master of ceremonies at a three-ring circus. Essentially, all of the variables that comprise a realistic work environment are set free at the same time, hopefully resulting in what most participants would recognize as a realistic depiction of their work life. The learning coach (who often really finds herself or himself in the role of an emcee) is responsible for focusing on two major categories of variables: the variables that can be directly controlled and the variables that can only be indirectly influenced.

The degree of difficulty that the learners encounter during a simulation or other learning event is directly related to the variables that can be controlled. A specific example would be providing feedback to role players in the simulation. For example, in the experience-based learning event for sales associates, the sales people must positively influence the chief financial officer (CFO) of a large financial institution in order to sell a specific service. By observing the CFO in action, the learning coach could provide appropriate feedback, and thereby adjust the difficulty of the sales calls by suggesting how the CFO should react to and otherwise deal with specific sales teams.

The learning coach can also adjust other variables of reality should a specific situation warrant such an intervention. These might include the success criteria for the learning deliverables, the total number of learning deliverables required, or even the time allowed for each activity.

Variables that can only be influenced relate directly to the learners attainment of the knowledge, skills, and insights that are the focus of the learning event. Adjustments that can be made include varying the amount of direct support provided by a process coach (or subject matter expert), the extent of feedback provided that is related to the deliverables that the learners produce, and the depth of detail covered during a reflection session. The learning coach must maintain a continual focus on assisting learners in their efforts to achieve personal and organizational learning goals. This requires that the learning coach recognize the differences between these variables that can be controlled and those variables that can be influenced and to guide the learning session accordingly.

5. Assessing the Results

Because simulating reality is based on performance goals that combine art and science, assessing the results of the learning event can be achieved with both objective and subjective criteria. The objective assessment of performance occurs through the evaluation of the tangible deliverables that are the outputs of performance. Subjective assessment occurs as a critique of the factors that support the deliverables such as: strategy, motivation, risk, creativity, and the like. Consider the law student who chooses a defense strategy, builds the defense around that strategy, and then justifies the rationale behind those decisions. So too can assessment criteria evaluate both the actual deliverable and the process used in creating that deliverable. Ideally, feedback is triangulated between the participants, the process coach or subject matter expert, and the role players, so that each is giving and receiving feedback on the others' performance.

Resetting Stakeholder Expectations

Resetting stakeholder expectations regarding the learning that occurs is critical to the success of the program. The fact that simulation means the total immersion of individuals into a number of possible scenarios that they may encounter enables individuals to choose their own learning direction. Each person is going to make different choices based upon their individual needs. A group of stakeholders, such as software developers, will come to the learning coach wanting to make sure that at the end of the learning event "everyone knows how to be proficient with their new multivariate analysis forecasting tool." To the extent that the learner needs to use this tool to accomplish their goals, they will be able to use it. However, proficiency becomes an individual choice and not one that can be "guaranteed" for the entire group. Stakeholder expectations need to be reset accordingly. The results that learning coaches guarantee to stakeholders is that learners will attain new knowledge, develop new skills, and acquire valuable insights within the context of what they have to do every day at work. They will learn how to learn, and this is the true gift of fast cycle, experienced-based learning.

CONCLUSION

Experience-based learning is a special type of learning approach designed to support art and science learning requirements. By providing the learners with a goal, support resources, and coaching, the learners' knowledge, skills, and insight are developed while working toward the achievement of the goal. Having such a performance focus—rather than a "right answer" focus found in traditional learning events—allows learners to learn in a way that is natural to them, in an environment that is natural to them. More importantly, experience-based learning provides learners with the ability to learn how to learn, which will ultimately be what they use the most the next Monday morning.

The Coaching Roundabout: A Personal Narrative About Helping Executives Lead Change

Dick Richards

For OD professionals, coaching an executive or manager who is leading organizational change is very much like navigating the traffic circles called "roundabouts" that are so ubiquitous along British highways. In Britain, a driver who knows where he or she is headed enters an unfamiliar roundabout and drives around the circle looking for a sign pointing to a target, usually a village or region, lying between the roundabout and the ultimate destination. The driver then proceeds from roundabout to roundabout, from target to target, until reaching the ultimate destination. Getting to that ultimate destination requires some idea of what intermediate targets to head for.

Coaching for executives and managers has become a considerably popular and potent tool. It has many advantages. It responds to the demands of the current business universe. It occurs in work time rather than days of training away from the business. It focuses on the very real and very live issues of the business moment, rather than on training exercises like a raft trip on the Colorado River. It is highly personalized and customized, and so can be right on the mark for the individual. It accelerates learning.

The ultimate destination of such coaching enables the executive or manager to guide the change process in a way that makes best use of who he or she is, that is most personally fulfilling, and that is best for the organization. Getting there, like getting from London to Land's End by car, requires knowing the intermediate targets.

In coaching executives and managers who are challenged by the need to facilitate rapid change, four crucial roundabouts are targeted:

- Speaking from the heart.
- Framing an authentic role.
- Making good use of your life.
- Aligning behavior with intention.

SPEAKING FROM THE HEART

In a restaurant in Atlanta, I have dinner with the regional head of sales for a giant financial services company. I am his coach. We are preparing for a meeting tomorrow. He is expected to deliver an urgent message to about 250 people. The message, honed in the company's headquarters, is being delivered by people like him throughout the company. The message goes something like this:

> We are not doing well. The competition is passing us. We have lost sight of our customers. We have lost their trust and must reclaim it. We have to stop obsessing over our internal skirmishes, pull together, and make things work for the people we serve. We have little time; we must act now.

Those are the things he is expected to say, and he seems ready to say them, seems even to believe them. After we review those sobering messages and once we are confident that he has the script down pat, he relaxes over dinner.

"You know," he tells me, "I cannot fathom how we lost sight of the fact that what we do is help our customers fulfill their dreams." He pauses, shakes his head sadly, and says, "That is what we are supposed to do, you know. We are supposed to help people fulfill their dreams. Their financial dreams, at least. That is what our customers expect of us. It is why they pay us."

The way he speaks this second message, the message that emanates from himself rather than from corporate headquarters, is qualitatively different. It is not that the message from headquarters is wrong, but that this latter message comes from his heart rather than from the pages of script that he has received by e-mail. His tone of voice is different. It is at once more thoughtful and more passionate. It resonates more from who he is as a person, rather than from his title as a Manager of Sales.

"I hope you will say that tomorrow," I tell him. He looks surprised, places his knife and fork on the plate in front of him, rests his hands on the table, and looks directly at me.

"You think I should?" he asks.

"Absolutely," I tell him. "The logic of what your people must do is irrefutable: Pay attention to what customers want. Who today can argue with that message? But the passion, the caring about it, has to come from your people, and that can start with you. This business of 'helping people fulfill their dreams'—this is what matters to you. I could hear it in your voice just a moment ago. This is the arena in which you can take leadership. It is what you care about. I urge you to take responsibility for what you care about. Tell people about it. Tell the people tomorrow."

He seemed doubtful at dinner, unsure that his own words, expressing his thoughts and feelings, were fit to broadcast. But the next day, in the midst of delivering the message from headquarters, he paused to tell the assemblage how he felt about the dreams of their customers. There was not a sound in the room except for his voice. When he finished, the people in the room hesitated to speak or whisper among themselves, not quite believing what they had just heard, not quite believing that an executive of their firm cared in such a heartfelt way about the dreams of their customers, and was willing to say so. After this moment of stunned silence, a moment during which the executive looked around the room nervously for some sign that he had succeeded—or failed—the entire room erupted in applause.

Speaking from the heart means finding declarations that are resonant for one's self and that also forward the action in the organization's change process. Coaches can listen for those messages. They are often expressed in unguarded moments such as over dinner with a client or at a break during a training meeting. They are only expressed after some measure of trust has been established between the coach and the person being coached.

FRAMING AN AUTHENTIC ROLE

He is the CEO of a foreign division for a large computer company. He is one of those executives who is sent in to clean up wretched situations, and throughout his career he has been very successful at doing this. His way of improving these situations is, in his own words, to "kick butt." One member of his management team describes him as "abusive." Many members of his management team are afraid of him. He is not the kind of executive who ordinarily asks for help from a consultant, and he has not asked for personal coaching but for help with his management team. Still, it seems an odd request from someone seemingly as certain and gruff as he.

We talk for some time about the other members of his team, and he tells me what he would like me to do for each of them. So-and-so needs to be more of a team player. So-and-so needs to pay more attention to our top priorities. He continues going down his list.

I ask him, "What about you? What do you need?"

He tells me that he was passed over for a larger assignment. The corporate CEO, his boss, told him that they would have loved to have his skills and knowledge in the new assignment, but his style had abraded too many people. The new assignment would have brought him home from his foreign outpost to corporate headquarters, something he very much wants because his children and grandchildren live nearby. The implication is that some people at headquarters prefer he be kept at a distance—but his boss made it plain and clear, telling him that his style, although useful to the company, had become career limiting. Now he wants to find a new way.

The division under his stewardship is doing well. He has turned it around. His management team seems competent and dedicated. He tells me he has achieved this with his usual brand of "butt kicking," which he also calls "tough love."

I ask him if that is how he raised his children, practicing tough love. He tells me it was. I ask him how he is with his grandchildren. He says, "Oh, that is a totally different story. I am much more relaxed with them. I spend my time with them enjoying them and helping them learn."

I tell him, "Maybe you could be more that way with the people around you. Less a 'tough love' kind of manager, more like a grandparent. Maybe you could be more relaxed with them, enjoy them more, and focus on helping them learn."

He agrees to try that. I agree to help him, and two years later he is awarded the assignment he wanted in headquarters.

Framing an authentic role—tough-love father, grandfather, earth mother, and the like—allows us to bring an entire set of behaviors to a situation that is congruent with both ourselves and the requirements of the situation. It means uncovering some existing part of the self, not learning new behavior. Too often we all bring misconceptions or unproductive habits to our various life roles. We behave in stereotypical ways or ways that do not serve us well, nor the people around us. Executives and managers are particularly prone to these mistakes because we have so many preconceived notions about how they are supposed to be.

MAKING GOOD USE OF YOUR LIFE

He is a product line manager in a South American affiliate of a large computer products company. His primary reporting relationship is to a corporate product line manager in the United States. He is also a member of the affiliate's management team.

There appears to be much to be gained by cooperation with other product line managers on the management team. There may be opportunities to bundle his products with others in order to approach customers more effectively—and with less duplication of effort. Customers are complaining about being approached by too many sales people from his company representing different product lines. Because of the organizational structure, however, he has little financial incentive to cooperate with other product line managers.

His regional manager, the senior person on the management team, encourages such cooperation but with not much effect. The rewards come from the product line, not the region.

During a coaching session, I ask him one of the standard questions that I use to understand who he is, "Why is being in this job a good use of your life?"

He tells me that the most exciting part of his work is that he has the opportunity to use the resources of a huge multinational corporation to improve the standard of living in his country. As we talk about this, it becomes apparent to him that he could better achieve that end by cooperating with the other product line managers, even if the rewards to him are not immediately apparent.

Making good use of your life means understanding your broader vision, the reasons you are doing what you are doing that extend beyond your own self-interest. This understanding can become a powerful beacon to guide decisions and a source of declarations for speaking from the heart.

ALIGNING BEHAVIOR WITH INTENTION

She knows that her organization must encourage dialogue among its people. There have been too many years of creating nonpermeable boundaries between this department and that department, between the third floor and the fourth floor, and between levels of the organizational hierarchy. She knows that many of these barriers are getting in the way of serving customers and are creating an organizational climate of mistrust, antipathy, and gloom. During our first meeting, she tells me these things and much more.

She also knows she does not have all the answers or solutions to the many problems that plague the organization. She believes, however, that answers and solutions do exist and can be found if people would bring them to one another rather than to her. She wants people to take more responsibility for raising and solving the organization's problems. She intends to work to change all of that.

She calls a series of meetings aimed at getting people together from across their respective organizational boundaries. She wants them to share both their achievements and concerns with one another, to discover how they might act as resources for one another, and to cooperate in improving customer service.

The meetings go well but one thing about them bothers her. She knows there are problems and concerns that are not being raised. Fear has long pervaded the organization, and it is difficult for people to be honest with each other.

She has an idea about how to encourage people to raise difficult issues. She says, "How about if we give people blank index cards on which to write down their concerns and issues. Then we could collect them and answer the questions."

I cringe at this idea. "I don't think that is consistent with your intention to increase dialogue," I tell her. "It seems to me that anonymously submitting index cards will encourage people to evade responsibility rather than take it. It might also reinforce the notion that you have the answers."

She seems surprised, but on a moment's reflection she agrees. The technique she proposed, though certainly raising and responding to difficult questions, will undermine her intent.

Aligning behavior with intention is no easy matter when intentions change. We decide to strike off in a new direction but hold onto old comfortable behaviors. Someone, such as a coach, who can spot us doing that, or about to do it, can provide an invaluable service. When our behavior does not align with our intentions and we have gone public with our intentions, we sow confusion at best, and mistrust at worst.

FROM ROUNDABOUT TO ROUNDABOUT

A good road map of Britain will help us navigate the excursion from London to Land's End by showing which target we should seek signs for while driving around each roundabout: London to Plymouth to St. Austell to Helston to Penzance to Land's End. Coaches working with executives and managers during a change process have as their destination a successful coaching experience. Earlier, I defined that experience as *one that enables the executive or manager to guide the change process in a way that makes best use of who he or she is, is most personally fulfilling, and is best for the organization.* Driving toward this destination is not nearly as linear a path as driving from London to Land's End. Although we might know some of the targets along the way, there is no clear roadmap showing a succession of targets. The best we can do is know all the possible targets and steer towards them, keeping the ultimate destination in mind.

Each of these four coaching roundabouts—speaking from the heart, framing an authentic role, making good use of your life, and aligning behavior with intention— is both a target to be attained and more than one sign pointing to the next target. When we reach the region of *speaking from the heart,* for example, we find not only a target along the way, but also another roundabout showing us where we might go next.

As more and more organizations embrace the imperative of adapting quickly to change, they will require that their executives and managers change as well. This requirement will impel those executives and managers to seek the real time, work-focused process that a coach can provide. Coaches, in turn, will have to discover more and more of the important roundabouts to head for along the coaching process in order to serve both the person being coached and the organization.

PART V

Summary and Synthesis

CHAPTER 9

Putting It All On the Line:
Transformational Change at NCR's
Worldwide Services Logistics

CHAPTER 10

Lead With a Need for Speed

Putting It All On the Line: Transformational Change at NCR's Worldwide Services Logistics

Merrill C. Anderson, Ph.D.,
Melinda Morrow, and Rod Goelz

INTRODUCTION

In the past ten years or so, business leaders have devoted most of their energies to reducing costs. Reengineering, outsourcing, and downsizing have been the tools of choice to shrink the number of people, resources, and fixed cost requirements of organizations. Only recently has an interest in the "top line" of the profit equation, revenue, emerged. There has been a growing recognition that companies cannot "shrink themselves to prosperity." The key issue for many business leaders now is how to grow the business profitably.

The challenge for business leaders is to maintain the emphasis on cost discipline and yet make investments that are required to grow key elements of the business. Business leaders certainly do not have the luxury of time to sort out how to best meet these challenges. Organization development professionals are being increasingly called on to coach business leaders to work through a process to execute growth strategies, make targeted investments, carefully scrutinize business initiatives, and maintain cost discipline. The challenge for OD professionals is to create a process that accomplishes these objectives in the shortest period of time possible. In a time of fierce global competition, time is a true source of competitive advantage.

Accomplishing all of these objectives in a compressed time frame requires business leaders to rethink the business and transform the organization. Transforming an organization requires leaders to create a shared vision of the future; it requires employees to actively embrace change; and it requires a change coalition of leaders and employees to plan and execute organizational change. Transformational change is by its very nature a holistic approach impacting business processes, organization structure, people processes, reward mechanisms, and other elements of the organization.

It is incumbent upon OD professionals not only to coach clients to successfully transform their organization but to also demonstrate the financial as well as the nonfinancial return on investment that clients made in their transformation effort. Given today's business climate and the emphasis on creating shareholder value, OD professionals need to demonstrate how their work adds value to the business enterprise. It is no longer sufficient to merely capture generalized and nonfinancial benefits such as "improved communication" or "more effective team functioning." The contributions that OD interventions make to the top line (growth) and the bottom line (cost discipline) of the profit equation must be spelled out. This is how OD earns its keep.

This chapter presents a case study illustrating how transformational change was designed, deployed, and measured. The client in this case study, a distribution and logistics vice president working in a Fortune 250 company, was challenged by his CEO to find ways to contribute to business growth while improving overall asset management and cost containment. This case study will highlight how transformational change can be executed and how the financial return on investment in the change effort can be demonstrated. This case study tells the story of internal OD professionals working in a highly collaborative way with the client over a two-year period of time. Together the joint OD and client team:

1. *"Rethought" the business.* Critical gaps in the capability of the organization to execute its strategy were identified, and closing these gaps was viewed as essential to achieving the vision and transformation of the organization.
2. *Transformed the organization.* An overall change architecture was developed, and required actions linked tightly to the business strategy were implemented.
3. *Demonstrated value.* The financial return on the investment made by the client for the change effort was identified and communicated.

Each of these joint change activities will be addressed in more detail following a description of the client system and the rationale for organizational change.

CLIENT SYSTEM PROFILE AND CONTEXT FOR CHANGE

Worldwide Service Logistics (WSL) is responsible for the global movement of parts and supplies to support a $3 billion services business within the NCR Corporation. NCR is a $7 billion manufacturer of computer equipment and supplier of technology and professional services consulting for the financial, retail, and communications industries. WSL employs over 1,000 associates in support of 4,000 customer engineers around the world. WSL also supports end-use customers and third-party equipment maintenance vendors.

WSL had serious business problems. Their costs were running above industry standards and process efficiency was below benchmark results. Inventory turns were lower than competitors', which negatively impacted the overall asset utilization of NCR. To a large extent this was due to the lack of faith that the field engineers had in WSL inventory and distribution processes. Field engineers knew that if they kept the parts and equipment they needed in their trucks or homes, they would always be able to get what they needed. Trusting WSL delivery processes was another matter entirely. Unfortunately, all this equipment hoarding was eating up capital and reducing inventory turns.

The senior management team of WSL, led by a newly placed vice president, decided to hit these business problems head on. They also realized that a two-prong approach was needed—long term and short term—and that both approaches needed to be implemented immediately. Over the long term the leadership team realized that the vision of the business had to change. The future vision was to embrace an information management paradigm in which WSL acts as a broker in an integrated information network. The then-current reality of WSL was that of a physical warehouse in which parts and equipment were moved in a time- and labor-intensive fashion. This movement of parts and equipment was triggered by field-generated requests. It was largely a reactive process with little emphasis on assessing trends or proactively trying to determine what parts or equipment might be required to fix anticipated customer needs.

In the short term, significant cost reductions and improved process efficiencies had to be realized. The level of investment to sustain the current way of doing things was simply too burdensome on NCR's net operating revenue. The challenge that WSL faced was how to engage WSL employees in realizing an exciting new future, while at the same time reducing resources, reducing fixed costs, and placing added workload on employees to meet current customer needs.

The WSL leadership team engaged the internal NCR organization development team to help them successfully meet their business challenges. The OD team began work with the WSL organization and conducted interviews with many WSL employees representing the different functions, levels, and constituencies throughout WSL. The OD team and the WSL leadership team decided to utilize an organization capability assessment methodology to address both long-term and short-term business needs and create a solid sustainable plan of action.

RETHINKING THE WSL BUSINESS: IDENTIFICATION OF CRITICAL ORGANIZATION CAPABILITY GAPS

WSL's strategic plan represented both the long-term need to embrace the vision of becoming an information broker as well as the short-term need to stop the financial bleeding. The fundamental question the OD team posed to WSL leaders was: "Are you capable as an organization of achieving your strategy?" Moving from a "parts is parts" supplier to an information broker represents a dramatic shift in strategy and implies a dramatic shift in the capabilities required to realize this new strategy.

The WSL leadership team engaged the OD team to assess WSL's organization capabilities to execute its strategy. A three-phase process was utilized consisting of planning, assessing, and aligning capabilities to strategy.

Planning

The OD team met with the WSL's vice president to begin the planning phase and prepare the WSL organization for change. The WSL strategy was reviewed and documented. Communication materials explaining the strategy were developed and distributed to all leaders who participated in the organization capability process. The intention of this communication effort was to develop a shared mindset among all participants. These people needed to be of one mind regarding WSL's strategic direction and to collectively share passion and excitement for getting there. This effort also provided the conceptual foundation for assessing organizational capabilities. Introductory meetings were conducted with WSL leaders and others selected from other NCR business units, and the organization capability assessment sessions were scheduled.

Assessing

The assessment phase began by the OD team facilitating a series of sessions with the WSL leadership team and other employees selected from other NCR business units to generate a set of organization capabilities required to execute the strategy. An example of a capability was: "the ability to track trends in retail point-of-sale equipment faults." The leadership team and other business unit representatives engaged in spirited dialogue about what capabilities they needed to build to be successful. Twenty capabilities were generated in total. These capabilities were then prioritized by being rated according to two scales. The first scale assessed the organization capabilities according to *importance to strategy*. The second scale assessed the capabilities according to how well WSL *performed the capability vis-à-vis their competitors*. A two dimensional grid that displayed the ratings of each capability was established as shown in Figure 9.1.

The intention of this rating process is to ensure that there is alignment between how important a capability is to achieving the new strategy and how good WSL is currently performing the capability. If, for example, a capability is not that strategically critical, then performing at industry average is acceptable—and, in fact, preferable. This kind of capability would fall within the shaded band in Figure 9.1. If, however, a capability is extremely important to achieve the strategy but current performance is below that of the competition, then building this capability is in order. Building a capability requires dedicating resources and investment to make the appropriate changes to close the gap between current performance and the required future performance. This is referred to as a capability "gap." An example of this kind of capability would fall below the shaded band in Figure 9.1.

Plotting the ratings of all twenty capabilities on this two-dimensional chart allowed the leadership team to pinpoint capability gaps in their organization. It also provided a visual representation of exactly where work was needed to successfully execute the

FIGURE 9.1 *Organization Capability Assessment*

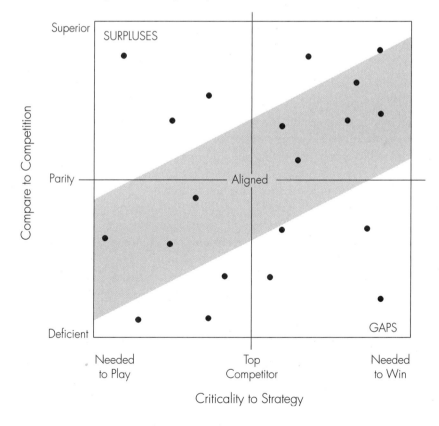

new strategy. These capability gaps represented their shared understanding of what was most critical for their strategy and that their performance of these critical capabilities was below par. For example, the "ability to quickly and globally manage distribution information" was rated as crucial for the strategy, and yet performance was rated significantly below that of their competition. This discussion then became a communication vehicle that was cascaded throughout the entire organization, thereby engaging all employees in making the needed changes.

WSL's performance on parts tracking by SKU, on the other hand, was rated as superior to that of competitors, but it was a capability that was deemed not to be that critical for the strategy. Performance closer to industry average would be acceptable and not compromise achievement of the strategy. This represents a capability surplus. The challenge posed to the WSL leadership team was how to direct resources currently being tied up on performing surplus capabilities to the most urgent capability *gaps*. In other words, move people and capital from parts tracking to information management. This approach also illustrates how the two tracks of achieving long-term strategy and short-term cost reductions can be accomplished simultaneously. Achieving long-term strategy is realized through building required capabilities, while short-term reductions are achieved through reducing resources and fixed costs tied up in executing surplus capabilities.

Aligning

The third and final phase of this part of the client engagement is dedicated to developing an overall change architecture for WSL. The phase under discussion in the previous section, assessing, revealed gaps and surpluses in twenty organizational capabilities. The issue now is how to weave together all of these data into an integrated and coherent plan for organizational change. In this phase, WSL leaders are architects charged with the responsibility to redesign the shape and substance of their organization.

The change architecture serves to develop actions needed to close critical capability gaps, bring surplus activity into alignment, and rationalize all other existing change initiatives with WSL. The intention is to eliminate all activity in the organization that does not either close a critical gap or bring a surplus into alignment. The leadership team carefully reviewed each capability and identified a crisp set of actions that encompassed a holistic approach to organizational change. Each set of action steps specifically identified implications for business process, organization structure and design, people processes such as succession planning and compensation, and how results would be measured. An example of how these actions were developed for one capability is depicted in Figure 9.2. A series of actions was described for all capabilities that, as a complete set, comprised the change architecture for WSL. The resulting change architecture presented to the leadership

FIGURE 9.2 *Change Architecture*

Capability Gap	Actions Required to Close Capability Gap			
	Process	Structure	People	Rewards
1. The ability to track trends in retail point-of-sale equipment faults	Redesign tracking process to accumulate trending data	Retail field engineering manager: add "anticipating future faults" to position responsibilities	Train field engineering staff in fault prediction methodology	Set specific annual fault prediction performance targets and adjust compensation accordingly
2. thru 20.				

team a holistic picture of all the changes in all of the areas that needed to happen. The leadership team then worked through the integration, timing, and sequencing of the change effort.

Through the use of the organization capability methodology, WSL was able to focus resources in the right activity, discover where resources could be made available for more strategic activity, and in the end have a solid blueprint for change. This approach also caused WSL leaders to have greater understanding of the required changes and to clearly identify their respective responsibilities to bring about organizational change.

TRANSFORMATIONAL CHANGE AT WSL

The WSL leadership was focused and actively engaged in planning the transformation of their business unit. However, most of the 1,000 other WSL employees had not been engaged at this point. What was needed then was to actively engage the hearts and minds and energy of all employees to understand, embrace, and execute the change architecture.

Understanding the Need For Change

A communication plan was developed to ensure that every WSL employee understood the need for the change and how the change would be implemented. This plan consisted of messages, delivery mechanisms, and timing. Key communication messages were developed and approved by the leadership. These messages referenced the external and internal business reasons that were driving the change and emphasized the role that each employee could play in executing the change. The bottom line message, however, was to the point: "If we do not change, we will be outsourced."

Communication delivery mechanisms included a newsletter, formal and informal team meetings, facilitated question and answer sessions, videotapes of leaders explaining the change, and a "community of practice." The community of practice was an intranet supported "chat room" dedicated to change within WSL. Anyone around the world could at any time sign on to the community site on the intranet, read what others had written, share their views with others, and distribute materials.

The timing of communications was generally geared towards cascading messages from the leadership on down through the organization and then ensuring that feedback made its way back to the leadership. No one assumed that the mere act of sending messages out to the organization meant that true communication was taking place. Surveys were conducted to ensure that messages were understood and incorporated into the belief system of the organization. All communications reinforced the message of why WSL was making the changes and provided a rationale that linked the changes to achieving the new strategy.

Embracing the Vision of the Future

The communication effort had clearly established in the minds of employees that the current state of WSL was unacceptable. What was needed now was to engage the hearts of the people to embrace an exciting vision of the future. An employee survey was conducted and the results indicated that 85% of the people did not understand the WSL vision—or even accept the notion that a vision was necessary! Action was needed—and quickly. A shared vision package was assembled that clearly articulated the vision. A cascading communication and engagement process flowed through the natural line of authority and work teams to help each employee understand and embrace the vision. Comparing the future vision with the current and undesirable state of WSL produced the kind of creative tension required to energize the execution of the change architecture.

A survey conducted six weeks later indicated that 50% of the employees sincerely shared the vision. While this was marked improvement over a relatively short period of time, still more work was needed. Continued and relentless communications closed this gap even further. Management meetings, voice mail broadcasts, and electronic mail bulletins reinforced the vision and provided up-to-date progress on achieving the vision. Quarterly business performance measures also communicated progress. The survey was readministered four months later and found that 90% of employees understood and embraced the vision.

Executing the Change Architecture

At this point the organization had amassed a tremendous amount of positive energy for change. It was important to quickly focus this energy on the most critical change imperatives with the highest strategic impact on the business. Otherwise, this energy could quickly dissipate and the engine for change would fade away. Fortunately, the change architecture pinpointed the more critical change imperatives. Those critical few organization capability gaps became the primary focus of the transformation of WSL. Multi-functional and multi-level teams of leaders and employees were organized to build these critical capabilities.

The change teams developed implementation plans that were drawn from the master change architecture produced by the organization capability assessments. Business processes, organization structure and design, people processes, reward mechanisms, and other elements of the organization were all factored into the change mix. Building the capability to predict parts requirements on a global basis, for example, required reengineering the parts forecasting process. The organization structure had to be redesigned to better support this new process. Variable compensation plans were revised to better reinforce the new behaviors required to make this new process work. This team approach ensured that integrated and holistic action plans were executed by a broad range of employees who now began to own the change process and its results.

While these teams continued their work, the OD team provided three essential change-enabling services: leadership coaching, change-agency skill development, and resistance management. Leadership coaching was an essential element of the success of this change effort. This coaching was performed by the OD team and dedicated to developing a more collaborative leadership style. The leadership style of each manager was assessed, alternative styles were discussed, and each manager considered adjustments to her/his current style to develop a more collaborative style.

The WSL leaders and many employees had become, whether they acknowledged it or not, full-fledged change agents. The OD team embarked on an effort to develop change-agency skills. Leaders and those employees who were members of one of the change teams participated in a series of coaching sessions and workshops to build change-agency skills. Change-management concepts and application techniques were explored and practiced. Concepts such as change sponsorship, advocacy, and resilience were included in these sessions. A change coalition was formalized that focused these learnings and ensured that change management was driving business results. The change coalition was comprised of the WSL leaders and all employees who were on a change team. This group ensured that change management tactics were integrated with a disciplined project management approach. The human as well as the technical aspects of change were planned for and addressed. This group also provided a regular forum to jointly address roles and responsibilities for change, track progress, and highlight problems to be solved in a collaborative setting.

Resistance to change is as inevitable as it is a natural human response to change. Resistance can be viewed as a positive sign that people are beginning to change. It is not to be eliminated but rather appropriately managed. The OD team and WSL leaders jointly implemented a resistance-management plan. An important part of this plan was the communication efforts that were well underway at this point. An organization-wide series of interactive workshops was conducted that allowed people to vent their feelings, but also to understand why venting was a natural part of their change experience. Skill-building techniques were included in these sessions that allowed people to develop or extend their individual change resilience.

The OD team continued to provide coaching on leading change and continuing the communication efforts. The formal workshops had successfully concluded, and the impact of this change effort was beginning to be visible in the business results. For example, a critical fill-rate measure of order processing efficiency increased by 27%. The cycle time required for incoming parts to become available for outgoing shipment was reduced by 78%. The change effort was positively impacting the bottom line of business: the annual net contribution from WSL to NCR Corporation was improved by $6.6 million.

DEMONSTRATING VALUE: THE FINANCIAL RETURN ON INVESTMENT

The OD team believed that it was important to show financial as well as nonfinancial benefits for the WSL transformation effort. In this day and age of decreasing budgets for support staff (such as OD) and an increased focus on business contribution, the OD team recognized the financial impact of their work would be important. First, this recognition would demonstrate the rigor of the WSL change effort. Second, communicating these financial benefits more broadly throughout NCR would support securing additional work from potential NCR clients. Of course, nonfinancial benefits are important to show as well.

Financial Benefits

The WSL leadership team had tracked $6.6 million in benefits as the direct result of this change project. The OD team asked the leadership team to assess how much they estimated that the OD team had contributed to this success. Leaders estimated that OD contributed at least 50% to the direct financial benefits. Leaders also said that they were 100% confident of their assessment of the direct OD contribution. The project benefits were then calculated by multiplying the improvement dollars ($6.6 million) times the contribution factor (50%) times the confidence factor (100%) resulting in benefits of $3.3 million. The formula can be summarized as:

Estimated Improvement Dollars × Contribution Factor × Confidence Factor = Benefits

$$\$6.6 \text{ MM} \quad\times\quad 50\% \quad\times\quad 100\% \quad = \$3.3 \text{ MM}$$

Next, the return on investment was calculated. The net cost was determined by subtracting the total cost of the project ($.3 million) from the benefits ($3.3 million) and dividing this number by the total project cost ($.3 million). This amount was multiplied by 100 and then multiplied by 100% to determine the return on investment. Thus, the OD team demonstrated a 1,000% return on the investment that WSL made in the change project. The formula can be summarized as follows:

$$\frac{\text{Benefits} - \text{Cost}}{\text{Cost}} \times 100 \times 100\% = \text{ROI}$$

$$\frac{\$3.3 \text{ MM} - \$.3 \text{ MM}}{\$.3 \text{ MM}} \times 100 \times 100\% = 1000\%$$

CONCLUSION

WSL leaders fundamentally changed how they thought about their business. No longer did they view themselves as being in the *parts* distribution business but rather in the *information* distribution business. This fundamental shift in thinking led to the reassessment of the organizational capabilities required to realize the new business model—and building these capabilities required transforming the organization. The change architecture was the blueprint for transformational change.

Transforming the organization did not come easily. It required the hard work and dedication of WSL people and OD professionals: relentless communications, ongoing coaching, and an extensive series of workshops and learning experiences. The fruits of these efforts were tangible and had a significant business impact. The financial net contribution provided fuel for NCR's business growth. The organization capability process showed the leaders where to make targeted investments. Improved asset management took costs out of the business.

WSL had embarked on a new journey with invigorated leadership and an engaged workforce. The OD team felt proud of their accomplishments and honored to have worked on such a strategically critical effort with visionary and dynamic leaders. The change project, which at this point had spanned almost two years, created a climate culture change that was contagious—and for many in WSL this was priceless. Evidence of this culture change included a stronger leadership team, increased commitment of WSL employees to implement change, and evidence that the WSL culture embraced more open communication and collaboration to achieve their stated business goals. WSL had proven how to achieve business growth while shrinking costs and was well positioned for successfully facing future challenges.

Lead With a Need for Speed

Merrill C. Anderson, Ph.D.

S peed matters. A business may have a great strategy, but this strategy is competitive only if it is executed and if it is executed quickly. The global business landscape is becoming increasingly complex. Political, economic, and cultural events interact on a global scale with consequences that no one can predict. The assumptions that business leaders adopted when their business strategy was formulated can be abruptly invalidated by fast-changing world events. This means that the shelf life of business strategies is becoming shorter. Speed of execution has become a primary source of competitive advantage.

It is becoming increasingly the case that the *capability* of an organization to execute strategic change quickly determines business success or failure. Organizational flexibility is needed to make timely midcourse corrections in executing the strategy. Responsiveness is essential for the organization to quickly adapt to changing conditions in the environment such as shifts in market trends, competitive responses, or the introduction of new technologies. Agility is required to readily make internal adjustments in business process, structural design, or human resources practices in order to turn changing environmental conditions into a competitive advantage. And as the organization is buffeted about by internal and external changes, it is critically important that all organizational elements—process, structure, people practices, technology, and other elements—remain aligned to the strategy. Misalignments slow strategy execution. Resources are poorly leveraged. Market intelligence is not quickly acted upon. Sales targets are not met. Inventory turns increase. It is only a matter of time until cash flow slows and organizational sclerosis sets in.

Business leaders begin the process of building organizational capability by asking—and truthfully answering—key questions about the likelihood of their organizations successfully executing business strategy. Leaders may ask a broad constituency of employees and others:

> Are we capable as an organization of executing our strategy, and if not, what are the most critical capabilities we need to build?

It is essential to gain an outside and diverse perspective on how well the company performs these capabilities vis-à-vis competition. Customers, strategic partners, vendors, and other stakeholders may contribute their perspectives to the assessment. An honest and well-rounded assessment of company performance will reveal capability gaps. Leaders then must ask:

> How can we quickly close these gaps and build competitive capability?

This line of inquiry, explored through open dialogue, can energize people in the organization to dig deep within themselves to focus tremendous amounts of creative energy on building organization capability.

Building organization capabilities represents an ongoing and long-term commitment to invest in the organization and ensure that everyone's actions are in alignment with business strategy. This takes time. Unfortunately, the relentless pressure of achieving short-term financial results encourages leaders to reach for the "silver bullet" solution. There is hope that one bold act will reassure the investment community and inspire others to achieve business results. Downsizing, rightsizing, restructuring, and outsourcing have been the solutions of choice for leaders who value the *appearance* of action over creation of substance. Moreover, the announcements of these kinds of actions no longer mollify investors. People who are considering investing in a company are more influenced by the promise of the future than the accomplishments of the past. Market capitalization is becoming increasingly driven by the prospects for growth and the faith that investors place in leadership to deliver this business growth. Building organization capability for renewal and growth is the primary role for leaders.

Accepting this role of building organizational capability represents a dramatic shift for many business leaders. Following the analogy of a sailing vessel, leaders need to see their role more as the naval *architect* and less as the ship *captain*. Leaders, like naval architects, need to focus their attention on structural design and capability and appropriately delegate operating the helm and managing the map room to others. Designing an organization to be able to operate quickly, be responsive to emerging customer needs, be agile in making midcourse corrections and have all elements of the organization aligned to strategy is essential for business success. This represents the real work of today's business leader.

The preceding chapter illustrated how the leaders of the Worldwide Services Logistics organization embraced the role of organizational architect and engaged their employees to quickly execute their new business strategy. This effort began by having the leaders frankly assess the capability of their organization to execute the new strategy. Leaders critically evaluated the capability gaps and then set out to close these gaps. An example of a capability gap was their inability to accurately track trends in retail point-of-sale equipment faults. Closing these gaps resulted in an organization that was far more responsive to customer needs. Change management workshops were extensively conducted to help employees better understand how to successfully manage large-scale change. These learning efforts enabled WSL employees to be much more flexible in making midcourse adjustments required to execute the strategy successfully. This case study serves as an example of how leaders focused on building organization capability while employees "piloted the ship" and managed the day-to-day operations of making the strategy happen.

The WSL case study also highlighted the importance of addressing strategic change at *all* three levels: individual, team. and organization. Coaching individual leaders, conducting change management workshops for work teams, and conducting organization capability assessments were essential elements in the total strategic change picture. It is quite likely that, had any one of these elements been missing, the change effort would not have been successful. It is essential for those who are leading major organizational change to ensure that change interventions are adequately addressed at the individual, team, and organizational levels.

Chapter 4 provides another illustrative example of how a leadership team played the role of architect in rapidly designing a new shared-service organization. Key design features were agreed upon and then used to guide the design of critical capabilities of the new organization. An overall vision guided the design, but it was not until the design was complete that the vision really took shape. This vision enabled the leadership team to quickly build a cohesive organization that was aligned with business strategy and to describe their preferred relationships with customers, suppliers, and partners.

Other chapters in this book were intended to show how strategic change could be implemented in organizations faster, more effectively, and less expensively than traditional approaches. Chapter 3 showed how search conferencing can accelerate strategic planning, while Chapter 5 highlighted the Kaizen approach to speed up problem solving. Chapter 6 discussed how to rapidly develop ad hoc teams. Chapters 7 and 8 showed how people's learning can be accelerated through fast cycle learning and coaching, respectively. The new fast cycle learning paradigm breaks the mold of traditional classroom training by providing realistic, learner-centered environments. Coaching, unlike traditional training sessions, is a continuous process that is delivered when it is needed most at a person's place of business. Coaching accelerates learning by dealing with business issues in real time.

Is there a "speed limit" for the pace at which strategic change can be implemented? Chapter 2 takes the point of view that there is an upper speed limit, although, like any process, there are opportunities for decreasing the cycle time of change. It is incumbent upon business leaders to relentlessly challenge these speed limits and push their organizations to accelerate strategic change as much as humanly possible. The chapters of this book highlight potential opportunities for leaders, OD practitioners, consultants, and others to reduce the cycle time for change.

The speed of executing strategic change does matter. It matters to people in organizations whose livelihood depends upon their business success. It matters to the customers and consumers who rely on these organizations for goods and services. Lastly, it matters to investors who value nimble organizations with strong prospects for growth. Winning business leaders are those who understand how to build fast, capable companies.

OD practitioners are rising to the challenge of accelerating strategic change by reinventing how they create value for their business clients. The cycle time to diagnose, design, deploy, evaluate, and enhance strategic change interventions continues to be reduced, while the quality of the business impact of these interventions has increased. Consequently, strategies are executed more quickly, a broader constituency of people is readily engaged in the change effort, and leadership teams are strengthened in the process. Organizations capable of rapid strategic change attract investors, and investors' confidence soon translates into increased market capitalization and—with greater earnings per share performance—increased shareholder value. As we have come to know from Wall Street, it is shareholder value that is the ultimate measure of business success.